Caroline Ticknor

**A Hypocritical Romance**

And Other Stories

Caroline Ticknor

**A Hypocritical Romance**
*And Other Stories*

ISBN/EAN: 9783744692465

Printed in Europe, USA, Canada, Australia, Japan

Cover: Foto ©Thomas Meinert / pixelio.de

More available books at **www.hansebooks.com**

# A HYPOCRITICAL ROMANCE

# AND OTHER STORIES

BY

## CAROLINE TICKNOR

BOSTON
JOSEPH KNIGHT COMPANY
1896

Colonial Press:
C. H. Simonds & Co., Boston, Mass., U. S. A.
Electrotyped by Geo. C. Scott & Sons.

# PREFATORY NOTE

THE author's thanks are due to Messrs. Harper and Brothers, and to the publishers of the Cosmopolitan and New England Magazines for the use of several of the stories contained in this volume.

# CONTENTS

# LIST OF ILLUSTRATIONS

# A HYPOCRITICAL ROMANCE

# A HYPOCRITICAL ROMANCE

IT was rather to my credit than otherwise, that I first became a hypócrite, since it was wholly owing to my natural amiability and unselfishness of disposition.

As I look back upon the first stages of my development in that direction, I find it in every way a most commendable deterioration which sprang from a kindly desire to please and to conciliate, and not from a natural tendency to deceive or falsify.

When Aunt Sophia, whose whole soul is wrapped up in music, came to visit us, somebody must needs sit by and be politely appreciative while she rendered Chopin and Mendelssohn, or interpreted Mozart and Schumann with that true enthusiasm which fails to recognize the foolish flight of time. All the other members of our family openly avowed their keen dislike for music, and quietly but speedily withdrew to distant corners of the house whenever Aunt Sophia began to play, leaving me to suffer patiently, propped in some comfortless armchair in the drawing-room, a most unwilling victim.

" I presume that it would be hard to find a more

unmusical household anywhere," Aunt Sophia would remark, sharply, turning about to find that one by one the members of the family had melted from the room, during some favorite sonata which should have held them spellbound in their respective places.

" It is a sad thing for any one to have no delicate perception of what is most beautiful and elevating," she would continue, " but it is utterly lamentable for a whole family to be found wanting in the highest attributes."

At this point, I would protest that father had important letters to write, and mother household duties which she must attend to, while George was obliged to study his Latin.

" Don't try to excuse them," Aunt Sophia would exclaim, " they have not an atom of music in their souls, and, when I have said that, I have exhausted all that can be said in their defense."

" But, Aunt Sophia," I would feebly venture, longing to follow George up to the billiard-room, whence the click of balls was wafted to me during the pianissimo passages, " I 'm afraid that I have not very much music in my soul, either." To which she would make answer: " Don't detract from your natural gifts, Elizabeth; you are quite different from all the others. You have the genuine musical temperament. I recognized the fact when you were but a mere infant in arms; even then you were appreciative, you cried loudly when I came to a deeply pathetic passage of Beethoven's, you responded instantly to the wild sob in the notes, so that your nurse was forced to bear you screaming from the room."

After such a rebuke, I would sink back into my chair with desperate resignation, and try to take catnaps while Aunt Sophia continued her interpretations, until callers or luncheon brought me the coveted release. Many a time have I sat rigidly against the stiff, unsympathetic sofa cushions in the drawing-room, sternly philosophizing on the selfishness of frank and truthful souls : apostles of sincerity, who would not pretend, though, by so doing, they could mollify all strife and bring joy and good-will to all mankind.

I was conscious of being in perfect sympathy with every uncomplimentary utterance which father and George let fall regarding the great composers; in fact, I felt I was probably more actively antagonistic to these honorable gentlemen than they were, for I knew enough of Aunt Sophia's idols to hate them individually. Father and George merely despised them as a whole, while I cherished one form of hatred for Wagner, and another for old Johann Sebastian Bach ; my forced acquaintance with them gave me power to discriminate in my dislikes, and I found Mendelssohn's "Songs Without Words" unbearable in quite a different way from Chopin's nocturnes.

And yet I had often unblushingly assured Aunt Sophia that certain pieces were "exquisitely beautiful," after having surreptitiously read some carefully concealed novel through the entire performance. This was a line of conduct which, I must own, lowered me in my own estimation, though I mentally commented that I was not untruthful in my statement, since, undoubtedly, the pieces were "exquisitely beautiful" to Aunt Sophia.

On the strength of my musical temperament, I greatly endeared myself to her, and was rewarded for my unselfishness by costly rings at Christmas, or pearl opera-glasses and gold vinaigrettes upon my birthdays, while the other members of the family were meted out the penalty attendant upon unsympathetic natures. Aunt Sophia sent them decorative cards, impossible penwipers, and gilt-edged diaries, or little painted picture-frames, which would not stand upright, and into which no pictures could be made to fit.

But Aunt Sophia also favored me with a seat beside her at the symphony rehearsals, which privilege I could n't very well refuse, and this, in the eyes of those at home, more than offset innumerable vinaigrettes and rings.

How I dreaded Friday afternoons! And how much oftener they came round than any other afternoons! If I could get up a headache, or go out of town, or in any way avoid the weekly ordeal, I did so with alacrity, although I never allowed Aunt Sophia to imagine that anything short of grim necessity could keep me from her side.

It was, of course, hypocritical to the last degree to make her think that she was giving me so much pleasure when I was counting off each number on the program with barbaric gratitude, and murmuring to myself, "one more over;" but, after all, if it gave her satisfaction to imagine that because the ninth symphony lifted her up to the seventh heaven of bliss, it was elevating me to the same altitude, why should I undeceive her?

I used to manage to get delayed, in one way or another, almost every Friday, so as to avoid the overture, appearing in good season just often enough to avert suspicion. As it was, I succeeded in convincing Aunt Sophia that the line of cars on which I was dependent must be in a deplorably mismanaged condition, and, in spite of my assurances that in a crowded thoroughfare blockades were unavoidable, she persisted in writing several scathing protests to the evening papers, headed : "The Grievance of a Music Lover." Whenever I was obliged to listen to an overture, I invariably had some pressing engagement which would not permit me to remain after the first movement of the symphony, so that, on the whole, my sufferings were considerably abridged.

Aunt Sophia was not, however, contented with having me beside her at symphony concerts only, but insisted that I should accompany her to recitals, oratorios, delightful little musicales, and many other entertainments of like objectionable character. Thus I had many rare chances which would have turned any lover of music green with envy, and of which I availed myself like a lamb prepared for the slaughter.

Do not let me give the impression that these occasions were entirely seasons of unmitigated suffering for me. No, I was able to extract enough pleasure from them, in my own peculiar way, to make my musical life tolerable, else I could never have been such a successful hypocrite.

In the first place, I soon schooled myself to a high level of mental tranquillity, which made it possible for me to close my ears altogether to outward sounds; in this blissful state, concertos and polonaises floated by me, and I remained unharmed; I heard them not.

I would sit absorbed in my own pleasant meditations regarding the proper treatment of an Easter bonnet, or the artistic draping of a party gown, for half an hour at a time, serenely unconscious of the orchestra, which might have interpreted anything from Brahms to "Yankee Doodle," without troubling me. Occasionally Aunt Sophia would remark that it was a pleasure, during the different movements, to watch the feeling of the orchestra reflected in a sensitive face like mine. At such times I could not help experiencing a pang of remorse, but I regarded it as only fair to my aunt that I should be the one to suffer for the deception, so I endured the pricks of conscience, and spared her the humiliating truth. I could not really blame myself very much, on second thoughts, however, for it was not my fault if Aunt Sophia, with her great powers of discrimination, could not distinguish between the reflection of a trio in B major and that of a new Easter bonnet.

After a while I came to find the music a perfect inspiration to me. If I had been worried or troubled by some complex question which I found it difficult to answer, I had only to give myself up to the influence of some stirring symphony, and instantly all was well, my mind would clear without delay, and the vexed questions would straighten themselves out at once. As I sat calmly by Aunt Sophia's side, one delightful train of thought would follow another, through a charmed sequence, which extended on and on until it reached the final squeak of the violins.

I planned Christmas presents for my friends, laid out my summer wardrobe, checked off my calling list, or thoughtfully reviewed my latest favorite book, or again, I faithfully recalled the numerous recipes I had acquired at cooking school, and wondered if they would turn out the same at home, or else went over my part in the theatricals which our church was getting up to help the cause of Foreign Missions.

From time to time, my chain of thought was broken in upon by long bursts of applause, in which I always tried to join, until I found that many choice spirits regarded clapping as something quite apart from a high order of appreciation; this knowledge was a great relief to me, and, ever after, I simply sighed and looked off dreamily into space. This method gave Aunt Sophia as much satisfaction as if I had rapped crudely on the floor with my umbrella, and was a great saving on my gloves.

I derived a good deal of satisfaction from the regulation house musicales to which we went (apart from the refreshments), as I could almost always slip away from my aunt's side and find a seat, either in a far distant corner of the hall, or on the stairs, where I invariably encountered several kindred spirits, also bent upon enjoying themselves. Often we succeeded in withdrawing far enough up-stairs to talk straight through, without disturbing any one.

At home, alas, I was considered thoroughly musical; this being the only construction which could be put upon my regular attendance at symphony rehearsals; and for this reason I was mercilessly thrust into the breach whenever any musical people came to the house.

" Elizabeth is the musical member of this family," mother would remark, with satisfaction, as she withdrew, leaving me to enjoy a new collection of Italian songs, which Cousin Louisa had thoughtfully brought forth from the depths of her Saratoga trunk.

Then father, aways anxious to give pleasure to his children, actually invited to the house rising composers and long-haired students of harmony with whom, forsooth, I needs must struggle through woefully tedious conversations regarding their pet theme, while strains of merry laughter harassed me from the frivolous groups about the room.

Even George, who should have understood me better than the rest, brought home with him from college prominent members of the glee club, and friends who played the mandolin by the hour, to whose performances the family listened resignedly on my account, when I should have so much preferred to welcome the most insignificant member of the football team.

Under these circumstances, one would reasonably imagine that I must have gradually grown veritably musical, but I did not. On the contrary, I cared less and less for a violin each time I heard one played, disliked a piano more and more daily, felt my aversion to a 'cello constantly strengthening, while my contempt for even a cabinet organ steadily increased, — and so on through the whole list of these instruments of torture, not to mention the vocalist, toward whom my attitude was still less friendly.

But now the retribution, which for the sake of poetic justice (not the other kind) should overtake all hypocrites, descended upon me. When I realized what had happened, I was for a time perfectly aghast; then I rallied, and made up my mind to face the inevitable and make the best of it.

Oh, ruthless fate! I had fallen in love with a man after Aunt Sophia's own heart: a man whose whole soul was bound up in music. Could anything more unfortunate have happened to me, or anything more grievously grotesque?

For a long time I struggled against my natural inclination, and did my best to root up such a misplaced fancy from my heart. I knew full well that I could never be happy with an intensely musical helpmate. Why, then, should I doom myself to life-long wretchedness? I would not. I would shun his society; I would not see him when he came to call. I gave strict injunctions to the maid to this effect, telling her that when he came she was to say that I was not at home.

But it was no use, my admirable resolutions vanished into thinnest air the very first time I saw him coming up the street, and, fearing lest my heartless instructions should be implicitly carried out, I ran down and let him in before he had a chance to ring the bell, and then pretended (alas, how easily I can pretend!) that I was just passing through the hall, wholly by accident.

I felt convinced that I could never be happy with him, and yet I seemed to feel that I should be equally miserable without him; therefore, since I was destined to be unhappy in either case, I concluded I might as well be wretched in his society. Then I told the maid to understand that, when he came to call, I was not at home — "to anybody else."

But I am getting along much too rapidly with my narrative. I have n't mentioned where it was I first met Winthrop; his name is Winthrop, Winthrop Van der Water; such a nice name; a happy combination of the best in Boston and New York.

But to think that I should have seen him first at a symphony rehearsal, leaning against a radiator near the wall, not far from where Aunt Sophia and I were seated.

I had been trying to make up my mind, during some Russian music, whether to have a girls' luncheon for Cousin Louisa, or a card-party in the evening, when suddenly I became conscious that some one was watching me, and I glanced up hurriedly to meet a clear and penetrating gaze which seemed to read my very soul and fathom all my frivolous thoughts of card-parties and luncheons.

Tall, handsome, interesting, he stood with his head thrown back, drinking in every note of that wild, crashy Russian music, as though his life depended upon the verdict of the orchestra. I knew him instantly for one of those genuine enthusiasts who prefer the concerts when there are no soloists, and who pay a quarter of a dollar and, with a dreamy indifference to having people trample on their toes, enjoy their music standing up.

I glanced at him once or twice during the symphony, just to see if my theory regarding his being a true devotee was correct, and sure enough it was, for he stayed to the very end of the final movement. I had intended to leave before the second movement myself, but I decided to stay just to test my own powers of perception in regard to musical types.

He interested me as a clearly defined specimen, whom I could satisfactorily analyze. He had a ponderous looking book under his arm, which he opened from time to time, — this was a score of the music, of course ; then he wrote something down with a pencil occasionally, — these were comments upon the rendering of certain passages, no doubt. I came to the conclusion that he was studying harmony, and therefore came regularly to the rehearsals, while he probably played some instrument with intelligence and feeling.

The following Friday brought proof of the correctness of my surmises, for my musical friend was there again, in precisely the same spot; and after that I used to see him there regularly, apparently wrapped up in the music, with his eyes fixed upon the score-book. Quite often, I thought I caught him staring at Aunt Sophia, and I wondered if he recognized a kindred spirit in her.

I could not help wondering if I could possibly learn to enjoy music in that way, and I began to endeavor conscientiously to enter into the spirit of every piece, but it was no use. Perhaps if I had begun sooner I might have succeeded, but now it was too late. The more I tried to be appreciative and sympathetic, the less I became so, until I really made myself feel quite depressed and wretched.

One afternoon, I went with Aunt Sophia to a " music at four," " camp-stool " affair which we reached somewhat later than my aunt intended we should, and earlier than I hoped we might, owing to a friendly motor on the electric car which refused to make the wheels go round for nearly half an hour. Aunt Sophia was very much annoyed, as she considers it an insult to one's hostess to go late to camp-stool entertainments ; moreover, she likes to have her choice of seats.

I don't think myself that it makes a particle of difference when one arrives at a camp-stool reception, for, go as early as you may, they have always begun. Some one is singing, no matter at what time the drawing-room is reached, and all the other people, who have apparently been there for hours, look up with annoyance as you enter and make an

unpardonable racket trying to sink noiselessly into
a vacant chair, toward which your hostess nods with
a pained smile.

If, by chance, you manage to slip in during an intermission, and are about to shake hands, and let
fall some cordial utterance, my lady puts her finger
impressively to her lips, as she points to some in-
strumental celebrity who is about to inflict himself
upon the assembled company, and with an apolo-
getic blush you subside uncomfortably into the
nearest seat.

On the afternoon in question, somebody motioned
Aunt Sophia to a front seat that was unoccupied,
and I at once slipped into the hall, determined to
steal up-stairs and wait in the dressing-room, I felt
so cross and unmusical. My escape was cut off,
however, by our hostess, who touched my arm:
"There will be some more chairs here in a moment," she whispered, much to my discomfiture,
and then who should appear but my symphony
man, laden with camp-stools.

"I want you to know my nephew, Winthrop Van
der Water," she whispered, and a moment later he
had opened a chair for me, and sat down in another
at my side.

I was about to venture some remark to the effect
that I was sorry to have lost so much of the music,
when some one began a concerto and robbed the
world of one falsehood, which, however, would not

have materially increased the sum total for which I am responsible already.

We both listened to the music with breathless attention, and said how beautiful and delightful each selection was. I would have rather talked all the time, but I pretended I was enjoying it as much as he was, and, indeed, I applauded one aria so warmly that he insisted upon clapping until he brought about an encore which served me just right.

He asked if I was fond of music, and I said, "oh, yes," and he remarked that he already knew it, he had seen me at so many concerts. Moreover, he said that he could tell by watching people's faces how much they were enjoying themselves.

I tried to be as truthful as I could, and replied that I nearly always enjoyed myself. To which he responded, most impertinently, that I must have perfect taste. At this point I was rather glad to have a man get up and start a recitative. While he was singing it, I determined that I would not admit to Mr. Van der Water that I had ever noticed him at the rehearsals, so, at the end of the recitative, I ventured that I was surprised to know he had ever seen me before, and inquired if he had attended the last three or four concerts.

Then what do you think he said (after I had seen him there every time with that big book)? That he regretted he had been obliged to miss the last three or four!

"Then you must have a double," I exclaimed, foolishly, before I realized that he was only trying to trap me into acknowledging that I had seen him at the concerts, after all.   At first I was inclined to be provoked with him for such deception, but, on second thoughts, I made up my mind to laugh it off. Laughing things off is even better policy than "honesty" itself, I find, for, if a thing is deeply important, it's the surest method of concealment, and if it's not, why it's the best fun.

Later, when the refreshments were served, I introduced Mr. Van der Water to Aunt Sophia, and we all talked violin recitals, and sopranos, and quartets, until it was time to go home, and he seemed perfectly absorbed in every musical topic that Aunt Sophia dragged into the conversation.

After that afternoon, we ran across him at almost every musicale or concert that we attended, and he invariably came out of the hall the same moment we did, and found our carriage for us.   He was so polite and so musical that Aunt Sophia was perfectly charmed with him, and went so far as to ask him to come to a poky little song recital that she was to give in my honor, as I was visiting her for a few weeks at that time.

He came, and found it most delightful (so he assured Aunt Sophia), though I think that everybody else must have had a frightfully stupid time.   Certainly they all looked bored to death.

Mr. Van der Water, however, must really have enjoyed the song recital, for he came to call immediately afterwards to tell us how much pleasure we had given him, and from that time he dropped in upon us very often, and we had most delightful times, except that he always brought the conversation round to music (and when he did not introduce it I felt obliged to, knowing how fond he was of holding forth upon the subject), while Aunt Sophia, as a matter of course, never spoke of anything else.

And so the long and the short of it was that we talked music, music, music, and very little else beside. Each time that he came to see us, I was dragged in more deeply, until I felt that it would be impossible ever to extricate myself from such a false position. For, had I not pretended to share his deep and true enthusiasm, and assumed that I agreed with all his lovely theories regarding the superiority of the musical soul?

At last my position grew simply intolerable. I could not go on forever making believe, I was not hypocrite enough for that, so I determined to make a clean breast of everything the next time that we met. And then I postponed my confession until the next time but one, and so on.

Finally, somebody sent Aunt Sophia three tickets for a Wagner concert; she was, of course, quite charmed at the thought of hearing nothing but this esteemed favorite's compositions for a whole evening, and in a moment of enthusiasm she suggested asking Mr. Van der Water to act as our escort, in order that he might share the treat in store for us.

He accepted, as I knew he would when he learned what a heavy concert it was to be, and, when eight o'clock arrived, we were all sitting stiffly erect in those luxurious seats which the first balcony of our beloved Music Hall affords, with our knees uncomfortably jammed against the seats in front, ready to surrender ourselves to several hours of unalloyed enjoyment.

There we sat, filled with different emotions: Aunt Sophia brimful of expectant delight, Mr. Van der Water apparently the same, while I remained silent and glum; the time had come for me to pretend no more.

After three long pieces, through which I looked as bored as I knew how, Aunt Sophia asked me if I was not feeling well. To which I replied, wearily, that I felt tired and very hot. Then our escort suggested that, after the next number, we might step out into the hall, where there was a greater supply of oxygen.

At the end of the next piece, I said that I should like a breath of air, and asked Aunt Sophia if she would not come, too, but she declined, saying that *we* might walk about, but for her part she did n't care to risk losing the beginning of the next selection.

As I stepped out into the hallway, I drew a deep sigh of relief, for I knew that I was about to free myself of a great weight, which had been slowly crushing me into a musical mockery. We sauntered to an open door at the end of the hall and paused, inhaling the cool breeze.

" That is the fire-escape out there," my companion remarked, casually.

" Is it ? " I responded, absently, peering through the doorway.

" Come and explore it," he urged, stepping out and offering me his hand. " It 's a good plan for you to know where to go in case of fire."

I followed, and we stood looking down into the darkness.

" There is no luxury like pure air," I ventured, inhaling a long breath and wondering if he considered it dangerous to let go of my hand, now that we were standing in a comparatively safe spot.

" Yes," he replied, apparently unconscious of the fact that he was crushing one of my rings into my little finger, " one does not like to be suffocated, even to the strains of Wagner."

I knew that the fatal moment had arrived. " Do you think me so devoted to Wagner ? " I questioned, faintly.

" Oh, I 'm quite sure of it," he replied.

" Then, know that it is not safe to be sure of anything in this world," I exclaimed, drawing away my hand. "Do you want me to tell you the sober, earnest truth for once, — I hate Wagner — hate him — hate him!"

I could not see my companion's face as he stood by my side, but I could eloquently imagine his shocked expression.

"And not only Wagner, but all the other composers," I went on, chokingly; "I hate and abhor them all. I'm not really musical, not the least in the world, and I can't let you go on thinking that I am —"

"Is this true; do you mean what you say?" he broke in, excitedly.

"Yes, only too true," I went on, hurriedly. "I'm a hollow sham, a false pretender; I drifted into it all by trying to please Aunt Sophia, and it was so hard to make up my mind to undeceive you. Believe me, Aunt Sophia is the only one in sympathy with your beautiful musical ideas. I should be glad if I never heard any more music — never — never! Now you may despise me all that you want to," I concluded, stepping recklessly backward, and almost precipitating myself through an opening in the fire-escape.

"Elizabeth, dearest Elizabeth," he cried, catching hold of me, "for heaven's sake be careful, unless you want to kill yourself!"

"You might despise me less, then," I murmured.

"What," he burst forth, vehemently, "do you

think that I could ever do anything but adore you ? Nothing that you could possibly do would make any difference in my feelings toward you ; moreover, *I* am the one to be despised. I am the real pretender, not you ! I am the utterly unscrupulous deceiver. Your little, harmless pretenses were but the sweet sacrificing of your own preferences to another's, but mine were all put forth to gain my own selfish ends, to make you care for me. Oh, Elizabeth, I am not a whit more musical than you are ! "

It was my turn now to stand mute with astonishment while he went on.

" All my enthusiasm for music was just put on to please you. Those were law books, and never scores of the symphonies, you saw me carry. I would not go across the street for all the old composers in the world ! Do you suppose that I would have stood through all those tedious concerts, except to look at you ? I don't care a straw for the most superb performance — I only care for —"

But why should I chronicle anything so personal as the confession of the second hypocrite ?

Aunt Sophia was vexed enough with us for staying away so long ; she said, moreover, that she could not understand how anything short of a dead faint could have kept us outside during the three most beautiful selections on the program. She added, severely, that we had lost the " Fire Music ; "

but my companion whispered that we had found something infinitely better, namely, the fire-escape.

All the family are delighted that Winthrop is not musical, but Aunt Sophia cannot forgive him as yet. She persists in maintaining that I was always intensely musical until I fell in love with a hypocritical young man, who first won my affections by his false pretensions, and then used his wickedly acquired influence to destroy that quality of artistic appreciation which she had been years implanting in my soul.

# THE FATE OF CLYDE MOOR-FIELD, YACHTSMAN

# THE FATE OF CLYDE MOOR-FIELD, YACHTSMAN

THERE were two things, besides himself, of which Clyde Moorfield was passionately fond, and these were yachting and young ladies. It was a lamentable fact that his two preferences were often hard to reconcile, because the young ladies who suited his fastidious taste were apt to care little for his favorite sport; nevertheless, he generally managed to find one or two who were first-class sailors and who interested him as well, though the combination of these two requirements often gave him no small amount of trouble. His definition of happiness was a fine sailing breeze, a boat built after the most approved models (one which could win him two or three prizes every year), and a pretty girl who could help him reef or be entrusted with the tiller from time to time.

He had been disappointed in respect to this last requisition so many times that he had come to make it a point not to become interested in any girl until he found out whether or not she was what he styled

" a true salt."   If, after an  introduction, he received
a negative  reply  to  his  invariable  question,  " Are
you fond of yachting ? "  he  soon  excused  himself,
and studiously avoided  further advances  in  so  un-
profitable a direction.

Moorfield had been studying law  so  assiduously
for two or three years that during the winter seasons
he allowed himself very little recreation, refusing all
invitations,  and  shunning   society  conscientiously.
In summer time, however, he tried to make up for
all this self-denial, and he usually succeeded in having a blissfully selfish time.   He knew that  he  was
very  selfish,  but  he  gloried  in  it ;  he  revelled  in
pleasing himself exclusively, and  he  did  not  care
whether other  people  liked  it  or  not.   He  would
not play euchre, nor help the  older  ladies  out  on
whist, nor  make  up  a  set  of  tennis,  nor, in fact, do
anything but suit Mr. Clyde Moorfield ;  and he considered that the sooner the majority of bores  found
this  out  the  better.   He  had  not  come  away  to
spend his vacation  in  entertaining people who did
not interest him, and he did  not  propose to do it.

He  was  handsome and lazy, and, in spite of his
failure to appreciate them  as  he should  have  done,
the girls simply adored him.   Moorfield was a superb waltzer ; but he  said  that " he  did n't  care to
dance in summer, " and only strolled into the  dancing  hall occasionally to look on, when  he  would sit
and converse with the fortunate girl who pleased his

fancy, knowing full well that she would very much like to dance, but never asking her to do so, because he did n't care about it.

He never took out parties in his boat, having a perfect horror of being surrounded by a lot of people who lost off their hats and screamed whenever the boat went about, and who brought lemons out with them to prevent seasickness. He had no patience with people who were seasick; and a girl lost all charm for him who was not proof against a ground swell. He felt no sympathy for the poor sufferers who begged to be allowed to lie down in the bottom of the boat; he only despised them.

The fortunate young women upon whom he smiled did not fail to appreciate the favor, and an invitation to sail with him was never refused, — it was too great an honor; morever, the lucky recipient of it always took care to be promptly on hand at the appointed hour, for Mr. Clyde Moorfield did not like to be kept waiting.

He had demonstrated this fact on a memorable occasion when one independent damsel upon whom he had showered much attention had kept him striding up and down the pier for a whole half-hour. When she finally appeared, she found him calm and affable as ever, and even more entertaining and happy-go-lucky than usual, so that she experienced a slight feeling of disappointment, having hoped to ruffle him somewhat by the delay, which none of

the other girls would have dared to inflict.  Nevertheless, she thought she recognized in this amiability
a greater depth of devotion to her than she had even
dreamed of.  Alas, her satisfaction was but short-
lived; for never again did Clyde Moorfield ask her
to step over the gunwale of his dainty craft.  He was
polite and even provokingly agreeable whenever they
met, but that was all; he never joined her in her
promenade on the piazza, never sat beside her in
the dance hall; in fact, he showed plainly from that
day that her society was no longer an item on his
nautical program.  But after that few girls ever kept
the imperious yachtsman waiting; and if by chance
anything delayed them a moment beyond the appointed time, they were profuse in their apologies.

Moorfield would sit lazily on the wharf by the
hour, talking to the sailors and splicing a bit of
rope, or fishing for perch, which he invariably pulled
in one after the other with the same ease that characterized his performance of every other occupation.
Here he would remain, deaf to all entreaties to join
picnics or go on long drives to beautiful cascades.

"Oh, Mr. Moorfield, do come with us this morning!" a delegation of timid voices would venture
some auspicious day, when there was a dead calm
and sailing was out of the question, — but without
success.  He would thank them impressively for
their great kindness in asking him, and only regret
that his sail required some attention this morning,

or he would mention that he must run up to town to get his rudder mended. It was an especial pleasure for him at times to stroll up on to the hotel piazza and watch the picnics start off, when he would seat himself on the rail and view their departure with an amused smile, congratulating himself meanwhile that he was not obliged to ride three on a seat for a dozen miles. He would watch the young ladies come down one by one, all ready for the day's outing, and would thoughtfully pick out one from among them, and say to her, beseechingly, just as she was about to step into the wagon, "Oh, Miss Bangs, don't go on that old excursion, but stay and sail around the outer light with me, instead;" and, ten to one, she would accept his invitation on the spot, and desert the picnic without further ceremony. It was no wonder that Clyde Moorfield came to fancy that he was quite irresistible (though he really never shaped such a fancy into so many words); for how could he help entertaining a fairly good opinion of a young fellow whom other people valued so highly?

It happened, at about four o'clock one very warm afternoon (that hour sacred to after-dinner naps), that Miss Rose Silsbee and Mr. Moorfield strolled slowly up from the boat landing towards the hotel.

Rose was considered altogether too young by the other girls, being only sixteen, but she could handle a boat almost as skilfully as Moorfield himself, and could splice a piece of rope or box the compass like any old tar; and so, in spite of her damaging lack of years, she might have been seen almost daily at the helm of a certain graceful white craft, while its owner sat lazily by, giving her points on navigation, as they flew across the harbor.

On this particular occasion, however, the sail had been less of a success than usual, for the breeze had wholly died out, and Moorfield had been obliged to pull home, three miles against the tide, with one great clumsy oar. Even the most fascinating companionship loses some of its charm under these circumstances, and the two landed, hungry and cross, realizing that dinner at so late an hour was an unknown and probably unattainable quantity, as the dining-room doors closed promptly at three. As they reached the office several trunks were being carried up-stairs, followed by bell-boys with umbrellas and shawls.

"Ha, some arrivals by the afternoon coach!" Moorfield ejaculated. "We're in luck, for they will have to be given some dinner; see, the door is ajar."

Their spirits rose instantly at the prospect, and Moorfield, tossing his cap on to the hat-rack, ushered Miss Silsbee into the dining-room with a flourish.

"Where will you sit, madam?" he said, bowing.

"Hush," she cried, warningly; "don't you see

we 're not the only ones in the room ? There are two people over there who will take you for the head waiter, in that blue yachting uniform. Oh, look, look," she added, "I really believe they think you are ! "

"Very well, I 'll have a look at them," he returned ; and before she could stop him he had pulled out her chair with all the dignity befitting the presiding genius of the place ; then, with a mischievous glance, he crossed the dining-room, to where a very pretty girl was unmistakably beckoning to him.

Had the light in the room been less dim, Moorfield's yatching suit would hardly have passed muster ; but as it was, most of the shutters had been closed for the purpose of getting out the flies, and in the semi-darkness peculiarities in dress were not easily detected.

The new arrival was even prettier on close inspection, having fluffy light hair and soft brown eyes, and possessing an air of distinction which made itself felt at once and compelled a certain amount of homage from all who came under its sway ; she also had, in a large degree, that indefinable quality known as style. An elderly woman, whom she addressed as "auntie," was seated beside her.

"Will you be kind enough to see where our dinner is ? " she said, as Moorfield approached.

"Yes, we've been waiting a long time," the aunt put in, sharply.

"I am very sorry; I will see that you are served at once," he replied, trying to imitate the respectful tone of the head waiter, and at the same time fixing his gaze upon the niece. Then he possessed himself of a *carafe*, and deftly filled their glasses, quite as if he were in the habit of performing this office three times a day. After this he walked briskly across the room to where Rose was smothering her laughter.

"Oh, how could you?" she cried.

"I could do more than that for such a pretty girl," he responded. "Now I'm going to see if we can't have something ourselves. I'm nearly starved. Suppose we walk through into the little breakfast-room, so as not to spoil the impression that I have made in my new capacity."

While the hungry sailors were regaling themselves in the small breakfast-room, Miss Lucy Wainwright was remarking to her aunt, "What a very handsome head waiter that was! I presume he must be one of those students we hear so much about."

"He did seem quite gentlemanly," her aunt responded, "but he wasn't very attentive; he didn't come back to see if we had everything we wanted."

The Wainwrights had come down to be with some cousins, who happened to sit at the very next table to that which Mr. Clyde Moorfield graced with his presence. When, therefore, at supper, he strolled unconsciously across the dining-room and dropped into his seat, resplendent in a boiled shirt and cutaway, Miss Wainwright grasped her cousin's arm.

"Who is that?" she whispered, excitedly.

Her cousin told her.

"Is n't there a head waiter who looks just like him?"

"Why, no, indeed. What makes you ask?" questioned the other.

"Well, then, I mistook him for a waiter," Miss Wainwright said, desperately, and therewith proceeded to give an account of her afternoon's encounter.

"Oh, what a joke!" laughed her cousin, "to think that you should have taken the elegant Mr. Moorfield for a waiter!"

"It was a very mean thing for him to do," the other said, in an injured tone,—"very mean and ungentlemanly, and I never want to see him again."

"Oh, but he is the great beau of the hotel!"

"That makes no difference to me. I can't bear him, and I don't care to meet him; so be kind enough not to present him to me, for I don't wish to be rude, and if you do present him, I *shall* be."

So it came to pass that several days elapsed, and still Mr. Clyde Moorfield had not met the lovely

Miss Wainwright. This was not his fault, for he had made repeated efforts in that direction, without success, for she was always disappearing whenever he chanced to come up, or always starting off somewhere each time that he joined the group in which she was. At first, Moorfield thought that this must be accidental, but he presently perceived that it was intentional; and having reached this conclusion, he determined to be no longer thwarted. It was a novel sensation for him to feel that he was actually being avoided — he, who was used to having people run after him on all occasions. He was accustomed to having his own way, and that at once; so he decided upon a line of action, and then took Rose Silsbee into his confidence, knowing that she would assist him.

On the following morning, soon after breakfast, Moorfield walked leisurely across the piazza and down the road, apparently bound for the village. He was hardly out of sight, when Miss Silsbee, who had been promenading with Miss Wainwright, said to her:

"You must run up for your hat, and come for a little row with me."

"I'm afraid that you'll tip me over," that young woman responded.

"Oh, no, indeed! You can ask any of the boatmen if I'm not perfectly reliable," laughed Rose.

"Very well, I will trust myself with you if you

will be very careful; for I am frightfully timid on the water, and always expect to be drowned."

A few minutes later they were paddling about the bay; and at the same time Mr. Clyde Moorfield was calmly retracing his steps towards the boat landing. Rose pulled energetically for a while and then rested upon her oars.

"Now I am going to show you all the points of interest," she said. She turned around and began describing the scenery and commenting upon the picturesque aspect of the old fort opposite them. Suddenly Miss Wainwright exclaimed:

"Oh, where are your oars?"

Sure enough, they had slipped into the water, while Rose was discoursing upon the beauties of the landscape, and now floated at some distance from the boat.

"What shall we do?" cried Miss Wainwright, in distress.

"Don't be frightened," replied Rose, encouragingly; "nothing dreadful is going to happen to us. Look, there is a man on the wharf, and I am going to beckon to him."

"Oh, but he won't understand!"

"Wait and see," Rose returned, confidently, and she waved her hand towards the figure on the pier.

Just then Mr. Clyde Moorfield might have been seen replacing his marine glass in his pocket. Then he stepped into his small boat and pulled rapidly

towards the helpless craft, murmuring, " Rose, thou
shalt have a ten-pound box of candy when next I go
to town."

" See, see, the man is coming," cried Miss Wainwright, joyfully. " How well he understood your
signal! I should never have known what you
meant in the world."

" That's because you're not a sailor," Rose
remarked, with an air of superiority, which filled
her companion with admiration.

In a moment more, however, Miss Wainwright
exclaimed, in a different tone, " Oh, if it isn't that
Mr. Moorfield! "

" Why, so it is," Rose exclaimed. " How very
nice of him! How do you do, Mr. Moorfield,"
she called out. " Do you see what has happened
to us poor helpless creatures? We've lost both
oars, and might have drifted out to sea if you
hadn't seen us and come to the rescue." This
was stretching the truth slightly, as the tide was
carrying them swiftly ashore; but Miss Wainwright
believed it implicitly, and shuddered at the dreadful
thought.

" And you told me that you were perfectly reliable! " she said, reproachfully, to Rose.

" Well, I am. Mr. Moorfield, come and stand
up for me. Oh, I beg your pardon, I believe you
haven't met Miss Wainwright. Miss Wainwright,
allow me to present our preserver, Mr. Moorfield."

"THE FOLLOWING AFTERNOON HE WENT SAILING ALONE."

Moorfield brought his boat alongside, and Miss Wainwright extended a grateful hand to him over the gunwale.

"This is the second time that you have been of service to me, I think," she said, smiling. She had forgiven him the first offence.

That evening, Moorfield actually crossed the dance hall and invited Miss Wainwright to try a waltz with him, thereby greatly astonishing all the young ladies to whom he had confided his intention of not dancing during the summer; they sat regarding him with ill-concealed amazement, as he guided his fair partner through one waltz after another, apparently enjoying each more than the preceding one. That evening, too, he asked the new arrival if she wouldn't go sailing with him the next afternoon; but she thanked him and said that she didn't enjoy sailing in the least, and could never be persuaded to trust herself in any kind of a sailboat; she added, moreover, that she was made seasick by the slightest motion.

Moorfield tried to convince himself that the expression of such sentiments was more than sufficient to extinguish what little interest Miss Wainwright had awakened in his fickle breast; and the following afternoon he went sailing alone, hardening his heart, and leaving her playing tennis with young Camden from the West. Moorfield did not take a very long sail, however, in spite of there being a fine breeze, but glided back and forth near the shore, where he could hear the voices and laughter from the tennis ground, in which he seemed to feel an unusual interest. Finally, he moored his boat and went ashore, just in time to see the tennis players disperse and to catch a glimpse of Miss Wainwright and young Camden strolling off together towards the grove.

Again and again Moorfield said to himself that any girl who could not appreciate his favorite sport was lacking in the most important feminine attribute; and day after day he sullenly unfurled his sail and sped away across the bay in solitary enjoyment of his beloved pastime. But somehow he failed to derive from it the usual satisfaction. He found himself continually wondering what Miss Wainwright was doing on shore; and even a spanking breeze brought him no consolation.

Then followed a time when, day after day, his idle boat might have been seen swinging at her moorings, while the owner went on long and dusty expeditions for ferns, or played tennis with the young ladies. He had always declared that he saw no pleasure in sitting on damp, uncomfortable rocks, and wasting one's time in merely looking at the water; but now he suddenly became an enthusiastic devotee to that harmless recreation, and was to be seen for hours at a time contentedly perched upon some sharply pointed projection, reading poetry to Miss Lucy Wainwright, who remained blissfully unconscious of the fearful and wonderful transformation that her presence had wrought in the young yachtsman. In the morning he would walk down to the pier and view his boat sadly from the landing, and then he would return to the hotel piazza to watch Miss Wainwright work embroidery, or to ask her to take a walk over to the cliff with him.

His subjugation seemed complete when he rode off one morning to a clambake, on the back seat of the crowded picnic wagon, in charge of the hampers and luncheon baskets, and sandwiched in between two small boys, upon whom he found it necessary to exercise all his powers of eloquence in order to keep the contents of the hampers intact.

Whenever yachting was mentioned, Miss Wainwright freely expressed her disapproval of it. She said she " could n't understand how any one could find enjoyment in a boat which was always tipped way over on one side, and which was constantly shifting over to the other side, just as one had fairly succeeded in getting used to the latest position; then the boom constantly swung back and forth, endangering every one's life each time it passed over their heads." She said that she " had noticed, moreover, that there was invariably either too much wind, so that the sail had to be reefed and the topsail furiously hauled down, or else the wind died out altogether, and left the pleasure seekers to toil ashore in the blazing sun, or to drift about in a fog." She concluded by declaring that she " never had an easy moment when any one she cared for was in a sailboat."

Moorfield, at such times, sat gloomily by, refraining from joining in the conversation. He admired Miss Wainwright very much, but he told himself that if it came to an absolute choice between any young woman and his yachting, the latter must have the preference.

The time was now rapidly drawing near for the great annual regatta, which was, undoubtedly, the event of the season to all yachtsmen. Moorfield's boat was entered, as usual, and in such perfect condition that its owner felt quite sure of winning the first prize, though he knew that the race would be a close one, as several very fast boats were entered against him. During these days immediately preceding the race, Moorfield seemed to have returned to his old allegiance; the piazza saw him but seldom, and the tennis courts no longer formed a background for his athletic figure, and the other girls whispered that Miss Wainwright's charms, although great, were not sufficient to eclipse the annual regatta. Moorfield still hovered about her in the evening, but early morning found him at the helm of his beloved boat, skimming across the bay and experimenting on the amount of canvas that she could safely carry.

If Miss Wainwright felt at all chagrined at the apparent falling off of the young yachtsman's devotion, she gave no sign, but remained to all outward appearance wholly unconscious of it. She seemed to enjoy the society of the other swains equally well, and took long walks with young Camden, who was always on hand. She was, without doubt, one of those calm, happy natures, which accept gladly all the good things offered to them without sighing for those withheld. She evidently enjoyed Moorfield's society when he was with her, but was equally happy and contented when he was elsewhere, in fact, hardly seeming to note the difference.

Any one, however, who had watched her critically on one particular afternoon, when a tremendous and unexpected squall suddenly sprang up, might have discerned an unusual amount of excitement visible upon her expressive features. The peaceful bay was filled with angry whitecaps, and the small boats came scudding home like mad. The guests at the hotel, grouped about the piazza, eagerly watched the few boats that were still outside in the gale.

"I suppose that Moorfield is somewhere out there," somebody remarked, casually, and somebody else replied, "There's no need to worry about him, he has more lives than a cat."

Miss Wainwright did not speak to any one, but

stood looking out from the end of the piazza with tightly compressed lips, and with her eyes fixed upon a tiny speck far out across the harbor. It was just supper-time, and the others all gradually drifted into the dining-room without noticing that one lonely figure still remained motionless in a distant corner, disregarding the fury of the gale, which blew her hair wildly about, and only deserting her post when the yachtsman's pretty white boat swung securely at its moorings.

That evening she seemed to be in unusually high spirits, and when she met Moorfield after supper, she greeted him with a gay unconcern which convinced him that she had been very little troubled by his exposure to the terrific squall. He resented her calm indifference, which contrasted strongly with the interest shown by the others, who crowded round to hear his description of his afternoon's experience, and he made an effort to enlarge upon his imminent peril, telling graphically how he had narrowly escaped being capsized, in order to draw forth some expression of feeling from her. His words, however, apparently failed to produce the desired effect, as she only remarked lightly that she "supposed that sort of thing was what a yachtsman enjoyed." He remembered that she had said that it worried her dreadfully to have any one that she cared for out on the water, and he meditated grimly that her attitude towards him had been clearly demonstrated. He persuaded himself that he regretted his devotion to so heartless and unfeeling a young woman, and decided that he had been rightly served for allowing himself to admire any one whose tastes were so little in sympathy with his own.

Moorfield pictured to himself at intervals during the next few days the probable result of an engagement between them (a picture which gave him more satisfaction than he wished to acknowledge), and he forced himself to conclude that they could never be happy together. Her first request would be for him to give up yachting, he felt sure of that. Yes, she would probably ask him to sell his boat at once. That was something that he could not do; he would never relinquish yachting,— no, not for any woman; so it was just as well that she cared nothing about him. Moorfield felt sure that this was absolutely so, as he dwelt upon her indifference on the day of the squall.

The days sped quickly by, until only one day remained before the long-talked-of race, and Moorfield, in consequence, remained on shore just long enough to swallow the amount of food necessary to sustain life, and actually failed to exchange a word with Miss Wainwright for over twenty-four hours.

The next morning dawned,— the perfection of a yachtsman's day. The sky was dotted with a few fleecy clouds, and a fine stiff breeze ruffled the surface of the water. Moorfield came down to breakfast in the highest of spirits, brimming over with that sense of good-will towards all the world which is apt to accompany the gratification of one's own desires. He saw, in his mind's eye, his boat flying through the water and rapidly increasing the distance between her and the boats following. As he passed through the office, Miss Wainwright was standing at the desk, and he fancied she smiled less brightly than usual, in return to his cheery good-morning.

"I'm glad that you have so fine a day for your race, Mr. Moorfield," she said, in rather a subdued tone. "When do you start?" she added.

"At eleven," he rejoined, pulling out his watch. "I suppose that you will come down to the landing to wish me good luck?"

"I should like to, but I'm afraid I can't."

Something in her tone attracted his attention, and he inquired, anxiously, "Is anything the matter, Miss Wainwright?"

In response, she pointed to a dispatch which she held in her hand.

"My father is ill, and they have telegraphed for me to come home," she said, simply, "so I shall take the twelve o'clock train."

Moorfield's high spirits suddenly evaporated.

"I'm dreadfully sorry," he exclaimed, looking greatly distressed. "Isn't there something I can do for you?"

"Thank you very much, but I can't think of anything, unless you want to order a buckboard to take me over to the station. I was just going to see about one. I presume I ought to start soon after eleven, as it is a four-mile drive."

"Yes, you certainly should start as soon as that," he replied, thoughtfully. Then he added, "But I don't see what I am to do without you. I shall be the picture of despair, I assure you."

"Ah, but you will have your boat for consolation," she returned, endeavoring to speak lightly.

"Yes, truly, I had forgotten that," he said, imitating her careless tone. "I see you appreciate the extent of my requirements."

"I shall have to go and finish my packing now," she exclaimed, hurriedly, "so perhaps I had better say good-by at once, since you will be off before I start."

She extended her hand to Moorfield, who grasped it warmly, and appeared quite unwilling to let it go again.

"I hope we shall meet again," she said, faintly. "The acquaintance has been a very pleasant one to me."

"I am just beginning to realize how pleasant it has been to me, now that you are going away," he said, soberly, while he looked steadily into her eyes, which dropped before his gaze; "and now that I *know*, you may be sure that we shall meet again, and it will be very soon, he added, with decision. "Good-by, I will go and see about your buckboard at once."

She watched him disappear, and then slowly went up-stairs, with a mist gathering before her eyes. When she reached her room she looked out of the window and caught sight of Moorfield wending his way towards the boat landing.

" He is sorry to have me go," she said to herself, "but he still has his yacht race."

At eleven o'clock, promptly, something resembling a swarm of big white butterflies skimmed across the water. The breeze filled the snowy sails and the foam flew merrily, as the many boats scudded swiftly before the wind, and the practised eyes of the yachtsmen sparkled with pleasure as they steered towards the distant bell-buoy.

Miss Wainwright, arrayed in a dark travelling suit, stood, bag in hand, waiting for the buckboard to appear.

" I hope that Mr. Moorfield did not forget to give the order," she remarked to her aunt, who was waiting to see her depart.

After bidding her aunt good-by, she glanced over her shoulder at the fleet of white sails, and at the pier crowded with gay spectators, and alive with flags and fluttering streamers which waved in the breeze; then she turned with a sigh towards the buckboard which had just driven up to the door.

As the driver jumped out and extended his hand to assist her, a sudden wave of color mounted to her cheeks.

" Why, Mr. Moorfield, is that you ? How very kind ! But I thought — "

She faltered, looking over her shoulder towards the flying sails. He made no reply, but helped her into the buckboard and sprang in after her.

" And you gave up the race," she murmured, reproachfully, " just to drive me over to the station ? Oh, Mr. Moorfield ! "

He laughed derisively.

" The race ! Is there a race ? I had quite forgotten it." Then he continued more gently, " Do you suppose that all the yacht races in the world are anything to me, when you are going away ? "

Before they reached the station, Moorfield had learned with much satisfaction that, far from being indifferent on the afternoon of the squall, Miss Wainwright had suffered untold agony until she saw him once more safely on shore. As the train came into sight, she murmured :

" Oh, there is one thing which I want you to promise me, Clyde, dear."

" Anything in my power, dearest," he replied, feeling that to give up yachting forever would be a joy rather than otherwise.

" It is this," she went on, hurriedly ; " I know that I am often very selfish, though I don't mean to be ;

and so I am going to get you to help me to try not to be so any longer. You shall begin by promising not to give up your yachting on my account. I want you to enjoy it just as much as if I could go with you. You will promise, won't you?" and she stepped on board the train.

"I will do anything to please you, my love," he answered, standing wrapped in admiration of this final revelation of her unselfishness until the train had steamed far out of sight.

Yet in spite of this promise, Clyde Moorfield ceased to be a yachtsman from that moment. His interest in his old pastime seemed to have suddenly departed; and at the end of a month he had sold his boat to a friend, who had several times offered to take it off from his hands in case he ever wished to dispose of it.

The other fellows said that Clyde was "very much engaged now," but declared that he "would get over it in time;" they gave him six months. At last accounts, however, two years had elapsed, and he had failed to fulfil their predictions.

Mrs. Clyde Moorfield often asks him why he doesn't go off on a nice long cruise, though I suspect she is none too anxious to have him do it; but he always replies that somehow or other he has lost his interest in yachting, and, what is more, he cannot understand how he ever could have cared so much about it.

# THE JUDGMENT OF PARIS
## REVERSED

# THE JUDGMENT OF PARIS REVERSED

I LITTLE thought that I should ever be called upon to fill the *rôle* of the world-famous Trojan, especially as I had always bemoaned the fact that I was not blessed with my full share of the good looks with which my enemy Paris was so plentifully endowed. I say enemy advisedly, for I disliked him from the first, and have always cherished a wholesome disdain for him, while I regarded his willingness to give up both wisdom and riches, merely for the sake of a good-looking woman, as the very height of imbecility, which could not have failed to bring upon him condign punishment.

Being an old bachelor myself, and blessed with what I considered a fair amount of common sense, I felicitated myself that so far I had not fallen a victim to the charms of any member of the fair sex. Possibly this may have been due to the fact that I had always avoided the danger, and had let the fair ones severely alone. My friends often tried to inveigle me into society, but I would not be tempted.

I was contented, and determined to let well enough alone. I would not court unhappiness, nor would I call upon anybody's pretty sisters — no, not I.

On a certain winter's evening, a little over a year ago, I had been enjoying a very cozy dinner with my three friends, Weston, Hollingsford, and Mitchell, charming fellows, who, though somewhat younger than I, yet always showed a willingness to dine *chez moi*, which was not tempered by any discrepancy in years. On this particular evening dinner was over, and Mitchell was just dropping a second lump of sugar into his cup of black coffee, when the conversation drifted in the direction of the German opera.

"Madame Flambeau is, without doubt, as ugly a woman as ever existed," I incidentally remarked.

"Oh, no," broke in Weston; "indeed she is not. I have a cousin, by whose side she would be considered a perfect beauty."

I hastened to declare that I did not believe it possible, when Hollingsford asserted that he had a cousin whom he would match against any homely woman that Weston could produce.

"I don't believe that your cousin is a circumstance to mine," he continued, enthusiastically. "She would take a prize in any exhibition, and create a sensation that would fill the heart of the ten-thousand-dollar beauty with despair. I have no hesitation in saying that she is the plainest woman in the whole world."

"Look here," interrupted Mitchell, who had, up to this point, seemed quite absorbed in studying the weather indications presented by the bubbles floating across the surface of his coffee; "*I* have a cousin, too, whom I'm ready to put up against any two women that you can produce, and I will wager any amount that she will knock Hollingsford's cousin into the middle of next week."

"Impossible," responded that worthy gentleman; "I'll never yield the prize to any one but Maria Agnes Palmer, only daughter of my beloved Aunt Mary, who always used to urge my mother to let me spend my vacations with her, in order that she might make my life miserable, until I came to regard the opening of school as a happy release. She belonged to Macaulay's class of old Puritans, who looked upon bear-baiting as a sin, not because it gave pain to the bear, but because it gave pleasure to the spectators, and Maria Agnes is just like her mother, so every one tells me, both in looks and disposition."

"I say, Weston," exclaimed Mitchell, "what fun it would be to bring them all together, and let Lloyd, here, decide who is the ugliest; then we will abide by his decision, as he is, of course, the only disinterested one. How could I, for instance, ever regard my Cousin Kate Mitchell with an impartial eye, when I remember how she comes to see my sisters just so often, for the sole purpose of telling how injurious cigarettes are, how very extravagant I am considered, and what expensive roses she heard that I sent to Miss Wellington on the night of her reception, which I attended, after having regretted that business duties would prevent my coming to her (Kate's) musicale that same evening — as though I could be in two places at once?"

"Capital!" cried Weston. "We will invite them all to dinner, and Lloyd shall sit in judgment, and the cousins of the defeated candidates shall pay for the dinner. What do you say, Lloyd? Will you refuse to face such a galaxy of beauty?"

I replied that, under the circumstances, I would come to the dinner with pleasure, though they knew that it was against my principles to mingle in feminine society at all, but I begged that I might not be forced to decide so weighty a question. I was, however, overruled, and before I knew it had consented to shoulder the responsibility of selecting the least attractive cousin, and had, moreover, said that I should be most happy to take the whole party to the theatre in the evening.

We finally came to the conclusion that during the dinner I should have ample time to decide which cousin carried off the palm of ugliness, and to her, when dessert came on, I should present a bonbonnière, which, in form of a gilded apple, should surmount the tray of bonbons.

"And thus shall the judgment of Paris be re-

versed," gayly exclaimed Mitchell, as he condescendingly pocketed a couple of my best cigars
before bidding me good-night. "Only remember
that you must escort the heroine of the golden apple
to the theatre yourself, after having shown her such
marked consideration. Ha! ha! ha!" he added.
"To think of Lloyd really accompanying ladies to
the theatre of his own free will! We must keep a
sharp lookout for the cousins, fellows, if we are
going to expose them to the battery of his fascina-
tions. Poor things! I hope their heads will not be
completely turned."

I joined the laugh with the others, but after they
had gone I sat down by the fire and thought what
an idiot I had been to allow myself to be drawn
into such juvenile nonsense. Was this all that my
consistency amounted to? Ought my good resolutions, long preserved unbroken, to be thus lightly set
aside for anybody's cousins? Should they prove
ever so repulsive and disagreeable, they nevertheless
wore petticoats and belonged to that class of cold
and heartless schemers whose society I had for-
sworn since the day, long years since, when my best
friend, Richard Jackson, had died of a broken heart,
and I had determined thenceforward to have nothing more to do with the treacherous sex. After
all, it made very little difference to me. Cousins
might come and go without affecting me in the
least. I had long ago become invulnerable, and

had learned coldly to pass the schemers by on the other side.

In less than three weeks from this time the night for the eventful dinner arrived. It was to take place in my apartments, as I had heard that my sister, Mrs. Winchester, was to be in town, and — happy thought! — knowing that she would expect to dine with me, I arranged to have her come and help me to receive the cousins, for whose arrival I now waited with much greater interest than I would have willingly acknowledged to any one could be aroused within me merely by the arrival of three very ugly women. It was probably the fact of their unusual ugliness that interested me so much, and I had several times caught myself speculating upon the probable immensity of Miss Mitchell's mouth and the possible magnitude of Miss Palmer's nose. I had even calculated in a scientific way the relative importance of these two given features. Admitted that each was just as ugly as it could be, which was the more important, a nose or a mouth? Both were quite necessary, but there had been times when I had felt that I could dispense with my nose; but my mouth — never. I was determined to be most conscientious in my decision.

This was the first time that I had invited any ladies to dine with me, save an occasional distant relative from the country, and my sister, who always condescended to spend a long and unhappy evening with me once a year. How much good advice she could get into one evening, and what unalterable opinions she had on every subject, from politics to laundry bills! No one else could be held responsible for her opinions; she entered the world fully armed and equipped with them. It was bad enough for women to have opinions at all, and even when they had the sense to get them from some reasonable man, they always lost sight of the essential points, and permitted every little personal prejudice full sway in the end.

I could not but feel, however, a slight flutter of excitement at the thought of receiving three of the much-avoided sex at once, besides my sister. I vaguely wondered if the man had dusted the rooms. I knew that women objected very much to dust. Whenever I heard it said that any woman was "a model housekeeper" a vision arose before me of some one wearing a white apron, who appears flourishing in one hand a dusting cloth and in the other a feather duster; who invades the peaceful study or the tranquil sitting-room, and with her weapons of warfare begins her work of devastation. She fills the air with minute particles, and the dust rises at her approach; she moves all the papers, and alters the positions of the pipes and match-boxes; then she takes down all the books, and rubs the dust into the edges with the cloth before putting them all back in the wrong places. I went over to the mantel and blew violently to see if it was dusty; evidently it was, for I sneezed. How stupid of James! I took out my silk handkerchief and switched it nervously up and down the mantel-shelf until I succeeded in knocking off my best pipe — just nicely colored, too. Women were a perfect nuisance anyhow, and had always made trouble for every one since the advent of Eve. Nevertheless, I could not control a desire to glance in the mirror each time that I went by it — an offence of which I am seldom guilty — and as I straightened my tie for the sixth time I was dimly conscious of a faint satisfaction at the thought of perhaps making somewhat of an impression in my *rôle* of genial host upon an invoice of femininity which had not been spoiled by too much flattery and adoration. I was only forty, after all, and if not handsome, my hair had not yet begun to grow thin on top, and my teeth were really remarkably fine; the genial smiling host was certainly quite my style. I knew these thoughts to be unworthy of me as a scholar and scientist, but we are all unworthy of ourselves now and then.

Steps in the hall caused me to take up a paper and assume a careless position in my easy-chair by the fire. My sister had arrived and also Mitchell, by whose side appeared the first of the cousins. I rose hastily and met them with great cordiality. " I am so very glad to know you, Miss Mitchell. This is my sister, Mrs. Winchester, who has kindly consented to preside over our little party, and who will, I know, have the goodness to show the ladies where to leave their wraps." Before my first guests had taken off their things Hollingsford appeared, accompanied by his cousin, Miss Palmer, and closely followed by Weston and his cousin, Miss Winifred Weston.

It was not until all were fairly seated at table that I succeeded in getting a good square look at the three cousins, and then I know that I did stare. Good heavens! there had been some dreadful mistake. I looked from Hollingsford to Weston and from Weston to Mitchell, but without eliciting a responsive glance. Then I looked once more at the cousins; they were all three young and very beautiful. Slowly the truth dawned upon me: I was being made game of; I had been selected as a fitting victim for an amazing practical joke. Once I thought I caught a faint twinkle in Mitchell's perfidious eye, which convinced me of the fact. I doubted if these were their cousins at all; it was impossible that every one of the three should have such a pretty cousin. I would give them no satisfaction, however; they should not gather from my serene bearing that I recognized any departure from the original program; so I smiled and conversed with the cousins one and all in a way calculated to show that I was perfectly at my ease.

Miss Mitchell was a brilliant brunette, with

laughing brown eyes and very rosy cheeks and dark
wavy hair; she was dressed in a gown of dark blue
velvet which became her wonderfully, — a fact of
which she seemed quite aware. Miss Palmer and
Miss Weston were both blondes, though of quite
different types. The former was petite and charming, with blue eyes, pink cheeks, and very fluffy
light hair; while the latter was tall and graceful,
with large gray eyes, shaded by the longest of black
lashes; she had a wonderfully sweet smile, which
disclosed the whitest of teeth; she wore her hair
brushed straight back from her forehead, and
fastened in a simple knot at the back. Her dress
was of plain dark green silk, while Miss Palmer
wore a charming suit of light gray.

Surely the enemy had invaded my very camp,
but I would give no one the pleasure of knowing
what a blaze of wrath I was inwardly stifling as
I calmly passed the olives, and begged the fair ones
to try the salted almonds. It was not that I really
objected to the pretty girls, but it was the principle
of the thing. My confidence had been abused, and,
moreover, the wretched men had dared to invite
their cousins to come and laugh at me in my own
house. Oh, it was too much; it was adding insult
to injury. But had those confounded fellows allowed their cousins to share the joke which they
seemed to be enjoying so thoroughly? No, I would
not believe them capable of such baseness. All

this indignation I smothered beneath a surface of politeness and gay repartee. Miss Mitchell smiled upon me most enchantingly, admired my pet etchings, and thought me " so very kind to take them to the theatre afterward." Miss Palmer looked at me with the frankest of big blue eyes, and seemed to possess the wonderful faculty of drawing out one's opinions and preferences for the sole purpose of showing how perfectly she agreed with them all. She seemed to have always thought just as I did on every subject, as nearly as I could ascertain; but ever and anon I fancied that I caught a significant smile passing from her to Weston, and once I felt sure that Miss Palmer actually winked at Hollingsford.

This was more than flesh and blood could stand. I knew that the color was mounting to my cheeks, and that my temper was giving way. With a supreme effort I turned and began to devote myself to Miss Winifred Weston, in whose gray eyes I discerned a sympathetic quality which somehow reconciled me to the fact that she was not either old or ugly. I found her so very sweet and interesting that I almost had forgotten that any one else was present, until I realized that dessert was upon the table, and just in front of me I saw staring me in the face, *one small golden apple*, which surmounted an inviting dish of bon-bons.

Conversation suddenly seemed to flag, and I

knew that all eyes were upon the fatal apple. How I wished it a thousand miles away, and guarded by the fearful dragon of the Hesperides! Miss Kate Mitchell's eyes were twinkling, and Miss Palmer's glanced mischievously, while Miss Weston cast a sympathetic glance at me, I was sure, and my sister, who had slowly recovered from her first mute astonishment at my apparently new departure, bent upon me a questioning look.

The unrivalled impudence of Hollingsford rose to the emergency. "What is this?" he cried, gayly. "Not an apple of discord, I hope. I see by the expression of Lloyd's eye that he is going to present it to one of the young ladies."

What a pleasure it would have been to have obliged Hollingsford to swallow it then and there! Had he told Miss Weston that I was to select the least attractive cousin, and present the apple to her? Now they were all waiting to see me give myself away, make a fool of myself, lose my temper, or do something equally unbecoming. My breath came rapidly; I reached out my hand with a nervous motion toward the apple, with a wild desire to seize it and hurl it wildly at the smiling and deceitful Mitchell across the table.

No, I could not give it to Miss Weston, and so make her think that I considered the others better looking, when they neither of them could hold a candle to her in any respect. But then, if I gave it to either of the others, I was pledged to escort that one to the theatre; to sit by her; to talk to her. No, indeed, I would do nothing of the sort, to be laughed at by Miss Mitchell, to be made fun of by Miss Palmer. I would give it to my sister first, and I prepared to murmur something idiotic about "age before beauty."

The pause was in reality a brief one, but it was a very bitter one, when suddenly an angel of light came to my rescue in the guise of Miss Weston, who herself reached across to the accursed dish and took the golden apple in her dainty fingers.

"If this is an apple of discord," she cried, gayly, "it is a dangerous thing, and we should beware how we trifle with it. Take warning by the fate of the first Paris, Mr. Lloyd, and do not call down upon your head the wrath of Juno and Minerva. The modern solution is quite different; Paris must keep the apple himself, and with it his dangerous opinions. Then," she added, presenting it to me with a smile, "when the judgment is reversed, and Paris, instead of Aphrodite, receives the apple, surely no one can complain."

I accepted it with a grateful glance calculated to convey all the admiration I longed to express, while I replied that "Paris certainly had nothing to complain of when Aphrodite herself bestowed so great a favor upon him."

It was a delightful and happy conclusion, after

all, and I rose from the table in the highest of spirits, which were not lessened by the visible shade of disappointment depicted upon the faces of several of the party at my having been allowed to escape so easily. I offered my arm to Miss Weston, coupled with the hope that she would accept me as her escort for the evening, which she did, and what a perfect evening it was! And that was the beginning of the end — yes, the end of my old bachelorhood. A year ago I would never have believed that such a thing could happen. It was wholly preposterous, impossible; now it seems the most natural thing in the world. What poor, unstable, human creatures we are, all of us! Still, if we must change, let it be for the better, as in my case. Mitchell, Hollingsford, and Weston had their little joke; but "he laughs best who laughs last," and Weston has lost his pretty cousin into the bargain. I don't know how she ever consented to have me. She says that she married me to get rid of me, but my sister, to whom all jokes are very weighty and incomprehensible affairs, says that it was a very queer way of getting rid of me, she thinks.

Among my dearest possessions I cherish one small golden apple, which I will never part with, save to one to whom, should she require it, I might return my treasure, vowing that Paris was right, after all, for it belonged to the queen of love and beauty, and to her alone.

# A LITTLE STUDY IN COMMON SENSE

# A LITTLE STUDY IN COM-MON SENSE

WHATEVER lesser or greater articles of faith we have the foolishness (or wisdom) to question, there is one to which we all subscribe. One which rich and poor, and high and low, adopt in pleasing unison; the wise man, in his wisdom, still adheres to it, and even the fool has wits enough not to despise it.

This is the doctrine of "common sense."

"Nothing avails you if you have not common sense," we hear declaimed at frequent intervals during our journey from the cradle to the grave. We early learn to reverence and respect it, though we may fail to doff our caps to age, or to be reasonably civil to our betters.

As we increase in years, we generally value still more highly "sound common sense," and fancy that most of the ills which have beset our pathway have crept in when this admirable commodity was absent. (And so, no doubt, they have.)

And when old age advances, we ever throw the weight of our experience into the balance with "cool common sense," of which we prate insufferably to all young persons, as though their chance of happiness depended solely on the attainment of this one desirable quality.

Most of the luckless beings who alight upon the surface of this earth arrive here in a very foolish state, and needs must spend the best years of their lives in fostering the little grain of sense which they have been endowed with at the start.

Mrs. De Forrest Bristol's daughter Juliette was not one of these. She came into the world, Minerva-like, armed and equipped with an almost incredible amount of common sense. She was born preëminently sensible, and at an age when other children behaved themselves (or misbehaved themselves) like the unreasonable babies that they were, she bore herself with an intelligence and dignity which quite electrified her parents and other relatives.

She early scorned a baby's rattle as a source of entertainment, preferring to watch the movements of those around her, while listening to their conversation. And if she did sometimes consent to bite upon a rubber ring, it was because she realized that by so doing she hastened the arrival of her least progressive teeth.

Juliette never screamed violently for " no cause whatsoever," as did her brothers and sisters in their infancy, nor did she show exaggerated glee over some brightly colored ball or painted top. She never made the entire household wretched because her dinner chanced to be delayed, or woke them up at some unearthly hour solely because her morning nap had been abridged.

She seemed to comprehend, without the least ado, that dolls were stuffed with sawdust, or cotton-wool, and to accept the lamentable fact with philosophic calmness; she understood that dolls were merely playthings and not alive, and, therefore, did not weep or make a fuss when they were injured or destroyed. No, she was far too sensible for that.

Juliette's keen perception early did away with myths regarding Santa Claus, whom she discerned at once as "only Uncle Charlie done up in fur and with a painted face on," and, after that, no urging or persuasion could induce her to hang up her stocking "just for a make-believe man to play he came and filled it." So she received her presents with the older members of the family, and was duly informed from whom they came.

The "fairies" and the mischief-making "brownies" she dismissed with a disdainful wave of her small hand, and banished "Mother Goose" and "Nonsense Rhymes" into the farthest corner of the nursery shelves, while pointing out to her surprised mamma that the "Arabian Nights" were "wrong, wrong stories" right straight through.

If at times Juliette disobeyed her parents, she invariably received the necessary punishment with an emotion akin to gratitude, because she realized that any chastisement administered was for her good.

When any of the other children slapped her, she never attempted to slap back, because she could foresee that, by so doing, she would provoke another and still harder slap, and so be worse off than before.

Mrs. Bristol never needed to urge this daughter to brush her hair or wash her face and hands, for Juliette at once perceived how much the application of a sponge and hair-brush contributed towards an attractive personal appearance. The necessary warnings which were fruitlessly bestowed upon the other children were never lost upon Juliette; she did not rush pell-mell into the dripping grass in her best shoes, or swallow quarts of deadly ice-water when overheated, or eat green apples, or touch "poison ivy" to see if it was really poisoned.

When she was eight years old Juliette protested that she must really be allowed to change her name to Julia; that seemed to her so much more sensible a name. She expressed much wonder at her mother's having chosen such a sentimental name for any child, — and Mrs. Bristol, who really was a very sentimental woman and doted upon high-flown names, assented, somewhat ruefully, to the arraignment of her taste in this respect, and to the substitution of Julia. Nor did she dare to own to her stern

mentor, that when she had selected the much-scorned
" Juliette " her wayward fancy had strongly leaned
towards " Hildegarde."

Julia grew up a most obedient and thoughtful
child, who could be trusted to look out for the other
children, who were several years her seniors, and to
prevent their getting into mischief.

She always carried her waterproof, umbrella, and
rubbers when it looked the least bit cloudy, and, in
consequence, was never drenched by unexpected
showers, although it was astonishing to note how
often the weather cleared, leaving the thoughtful
Julia to trudge home laden with the emblems of her
forethought not in use ; whereas, if it did rain, the
other children usually scrambled under her umbrella
and reached home quite as dry as she.

Julia was very much respected by her schoolmates,
as such a highly sensible girl must needs have been,
but she was seldom asked to share the foolish secrets
which delighted so many of the schoolgirls, or to
take part in any youthful escapades.   Julia, the
others knew, had too much sense for any such diver-
sions.   So they asked her to show them  how to
work their difficult examples, and then went off and
ate their chocolate creams and pickles with some
one else.

All the teachers held Julia in high esteem ; they
always knew what to expect of her and where to
find her, and were not disappointed.   She studied

faithfully because she realized that if she wasted her precious school-days she would be very sorry in after years; moreover, she knew that at her age the mind grasped new ideas more readily than at a later date, and understood that information then acquired would remain with her all through her life.

Miss Mills, the oldest teacher at the academy, declared that in all her long experience she had never come across a mind so logical and finely balanced as Julia's; she regarded her with steadily increasing interest, and pronounced her " a most remarkable young woman,"— yet Miss Mills's favorite pupil was Elsie Brown, a perfect flyaway, who never could remember where the lesson was, and when she did, forgot to learn it.

Although Julia was not the oldest sister, her brothers invariably consulted her on questions of importance, and brought her their torn garments to mend, appreciating her sensible advice and clever needle work. But they confided their youthful woes, their towering aspirations, and idle daydreams to their other sisters, who were not quite as intelligent as Julia, — and it was Rose or Winifred who helped to manufacture highly decorative missives to be dispatched in old St. Valentine's behalf.

Julia's brothers were very proud of her ability, for she excelled in everything which she attempted; she could throw a ball, swim, ride, row, or play tennis with the best of them, and seemed to understand just how things should be done, even before she had been shown the way.

Her brother's friends, too, equally admired Julia's prowess and held her up as an example to their sisters, but it was Rose or Winifred whom they invited to walk with them, or to go for a paddle in their canoes.

This certainly seemed a very curious mistake for them to make, for the young fellows knew that Julia was in every way superior to her sisters, who were really very senseless young women, foolish enough to fancy that the young men who took them out canoeing were very clever and remarkably fine fellows, whereas, their sister could have told them that they were very commonplace.

The young men all appreciated Julia's powers of conversation, for, after they had talked to her, they went away declaring that she was as intelligent and bright a girl as they had ever met, and if they sent back bunches of violets and boxes of candy to her sisters and not to her, it was because they felt that she was quite too sensible to value such trivial things.

Julia enjoyed remarkably good health, although in early childhood she had been more delicate than all the other children, for she had always taken the best care of herself. While her sisters were often very reckless about taking cold, she always went

provided with extra wraps, and her precautions invariably preserved her health, unless perchance, on
some occasion, she insisted upon putting her wraps
on some one else more thinly clad than she. Her
common sense, although it kept her well, did not
however insure her sisters, and so she often was
obliged to nurse them, and take them gruel, and
bathe their aching heads with weak cologne, which
was almost as tiresome as having some ailment herself.

Julia was always popular at parties because she
danced so gracefully and talked so well, and yet
her sisters usually got more favors in the German
than she, for everybody knew she was too sensible
to mind whether she had favors or not, while other
girls were very much provoked if they did not receive a goodly number.

Julia was, with all, a very pretty girl, but no one
ever mentioned the fact because all knew that she
thought more of intellectual worth than of mere superficial beauty, which was only "skin deep," and
bound to fade away in a few years; so no one
dreamed it would have pleased her to have been
told her "eyes were brilliant" or her "teeth like
pearls."

They saved such silly speeches for her sisters,
and talked to her of science, literature, yes, even
politics they could discuss intelligently with her.
And she had sense enough to recognize the value

of such conversation, though possibly she would have very much enjoyed the other kind, at times.

Julia would play on the piano for hours at a time while all the others danced, and nobody felt troubled, because all knew that she could play dance-music more easily and better than any of the rest, and was too sensible to mind whether she danced, herself, or not. Moreover, if the other girls were called upon to play, they would invariably expect some man to hover close to the piano to turn the music over, while Julia always said that it was much more sensible for all the men to dance, — and then, — she played without her notes.

There was one specially attractive man who seemed particularly fond of Julia, but she was far too sensible to offer him any encouragement.

He never would converse with her intelligently on any of the weighty topics which usually interested her, but revelled in a perfectly nonsensical discourse, which would have certainly disgusted Julia had she not had the sense to recognize beneath this flippant speech, a fine and sterling character, which reconciled her to a great deal of his frivolous conversation (and he favored her with a most generous amount). He used to talk to Julia just as foolishly as if she had been Rose or Winifred, and would make complimentary remarks about the color of her eyes, or the Greek outline of her profile, instead of talking literature, or ethics, as did her other friends.

Julia, who could not but feel regretful at the superficial way in which so fine a mind expressed itself, strove patiently to talk to him on more improving subjects, although her zeal was wholly misinterpreted by Rose and Winifred, who said that she was not so fond of talking sense as she pretended.

This young man even went so far astray from paths of common sense as to beg for a lock of Julia's hair, which she, of course, refrained from giving him, and actually stole one of her photographs from her eldest brother's dressing-table, after she had most sensibly refused to give him one. This she regarded as a dreadful piece of folly, but she had sense enough to make no fuss about it, and not to mention it to her two sisters; so the young man kept the picture.

When he came to call, he did not even ask to see the other members of the family, but told the maid that if Miss Julia was not in, he would come again some other time.

Julia was far too sensible to favor such a line of action and always called in Rose and Winifred, who did not know that he had specially refrained from asking for them, and freely took part in the conversation, not dreaming that he might have actually preferred to see Julia alone. At first, this used greatly to annoy the caller, who considered that he was being treated shabbily, but, after some little time, he became reconciled to Rose and Winifred ˙ and never failed to ask for the " young ladies."

This same man was extremely fond of chess, and used to drop in very frequently to play with Julia, who generally could beat him (she played so fine a game), and after they had ended a long and scientific struggle, he would suggest that, after such a contest, they really ought to step out on to the cool veranda to see the moon and get a breath of air. And she would readily assent, knowing that it was very beneficial to fill one's lungs with pure fresh air before retiring for the night.

Now, although Rose and Winifred did not play chess, they often hovered near and watched the game, and when the visitor suggested that they adjourn in search of oxygen or moonlight, Julia's common sense could not ignore the fact that pure, fresh air was also beneficial for Rose and Winifred, who in their turn had *not* the sense to realize that the young man might perhaps prefer a *tête-à-tête* with Julia, but joined the chess-players without waiting for further urging, which they undoubtedly would never have received.

As they inhaled the evening breezes on the cool veranda, the young man would devote himself to Julia, while Rose (who was invariably on hand) sat idly thrumming her guitar; she made a very pretty picture as the moonlight fell upon her, as both the others could not fail to realize, though Julia was the first to call attention to the fact. And the visitor, having once had his attention directed towards the picturesque musician, glanced frequently at her as he continued his conversation with her sister, and it was hardly strange that his mind sometimes wandered from the intelligent discourse he was enjoying, to Rose's fitful melodies, or that he even irrelevantly asked her to sing him this or that pet song, instead of answering at once some question which Julia had propounded.

As the long summer evenings crept by, the visitor's interest in Rose's songs increased, owing to the heat, which lessened his enthusiasm for chess (which never could have equalled Julia's), who would have played willingly (with him) no matter to what altitude the mercury had climbed.

Yes, the young man's interest in chess had certainly declined, and though he had declared, in times gone by, that he enjoyed this favorite game above all else, he now showed no desire to indulge in it at all, and, as they sat upon the porch, his conversation (which, I regret to say, showed little of the intellectual quality which Julia had endeavored to inculcate) was oftener addressed to Rose than to her sister.

In fact he hardly noticed that Julia often slipped away and left him there with Rose; or if he did, apparently he did not mind it, for Rose was very charming, although not intellectual in the least, and looked at him with an undisguised admiration which Julia (even had she felt it) would have been quite too sensible to have exhibited.

And so, at last, Rose and the visitor drifted away from Julia altogether, and she, seeing that her society was easily dispensed with, had too much sense to intrude where her company was not particularly desired.

Therefore it came about that when the young man came to call, he asked for Rose, who, not being sensible at all, did not feel called upon to urge her sister Julia to join them.

And one day, Rose and the young man, who had been so devoted to her sister, became engaged, and he forgot that he had stolen Julia's picture, or had considered chess the finest game in all the world, so much greater was his enthusiasm for music (especially that played by Rose on her guitar).

. When the engagement was announced to Julia, she kissed her sister, and extended her hand to the young man who had once wanted a lock of *her* hair, but when the latter gaily said that he should claim the privilege of saluting his future sister, she swiftly turned and left the room.

"I always thought that Julia barely tolerated me," the young man said, "but now I almost feel as though she actually dislikes me." To which

Rose, who knew her sister better, only answered evasively, "Never mind, she will get over it in time."

And Julia went and locked herself into her room and sat for hours at her desk gazing at a small package of letters fastened together with an elastic band (she deemed blue ribbon very foolish), which letters she read over slowly several times before she tore them up. After that she sat for a long time trying to convince herself that Rose would after all make the young man a great deal happier than she could ever have hoped to; but her good common sense refused this consolation, and told her plainly that this was not the case; so she sat motionless, and watched the scrap-basket where she had thrown the torn-up package of letters; but she was far too sensible to cry.

And Rose married the man who used to play so many games of chess with Julia, and no one ever dreamed (except Rose, and she never told the dream) that Julia cared. She was as sensible and practical as ever, and it was owing to her clear head and clever management that all the wedding festivities went off so smoothly.

"When you are married, Julia," Winifred cried, enthusiastically, after the bride had taken her departure, " you won't need any one to manage things for *you*, you understand so perfectly how everything ought to be done."

Julia did not reply at once, but turned and walked over to a long window, and stood there looking out for some time on to the veranda, where, in the silver moonlight, she had thoughtfully discussed so many intellectual themes with the young man who had just driven away with Rose amid a shower of rice. " I am too sensible ever to marry," she answered, quietly.

And so indeed she was.

# MR. HURD'S HOLIDAY

"'NO BUSINESS TO-MORROW, MY DEAR.'"

# MR. HURD'S HOLIDAY

———◆———

"NO business to-morrow, my dear," Mr. Hurd announced, cheerfully, to his better half, as he stepped into the sitting-room and deposited several brown paper bundles upon one of the chairs.

"Why, to be sure," she responded, brightening. "I had almost forgotten that it will be a holiday; what are you going to do to celebrate? I suppose that we might all go off somewhere for the day," she concluded, thoughtfully.

Mr. Hurd shook his head. "There are a number of things about the house which I am intending to look into to-morrow; it is only a few days ago that you were complaining that I was not more domestic, so now I am going to turn over a new leaf. I have come to the conclusion that we are constantly paying out money to incompetent workmen for little odd repairs that I could just as well do myself. Any man with brains and the proper tools at hand can turn off a good many dollars' worth of work in his spare moments," he went on, as he removed the paper wrappings from the several bundles.

"Are you sure that you are feeling as well as usual, Theodore?" his wife inquired, watching him in anxious astonishment, while she recalled her many fruitless efforts in the past to awaken in him a desire to help about some slight household detail which sadly needed attention.

"Never better, my dear," he answered, unrolling a bottle of glue and setting it upon the mantel-piece. "Why do you ask?"

"Well, you see, Theodore, it is such a new departure for you, that — I — could n't help wondering if —"

"Well, if what?"

"If anything were the matter; if you were quite yourself. You 're not feverish, are you, Theodore?" she concluded, running her fingers over his forehead.

Mr. Hurd smiled benignly, as he produced a small can of paint and a brush which he set down next to the glue. "I 'll tell you just how it happened, my dear," he said. "On my way down town I overtook Lovering, and as we walked along together I asked him casually how he was going to celebrate to-morrow. 'As I usually spend my holidays,' he replied, 'in repairing and tinkering up things about the house, and doing my best to freeze out the carpenter and the plumber, beside sorting over old papers and putting things to rights that I seldom have a chance at.' After I left him I began to think how many holidays I had wasted when

I might have been really accomplishing something, and have had money in my pocket to boot.

"I have reformed, my dear," he concluded, opening the last of the paper bundles, as you will see to-morrow; here are half a dozen new tools which I find I need if I am to do anything of this kind really well. Is n't that a nice little hammer? and you remember that we had n't any chisel or screw-driver that a man could properly work with."

Mrs. Hurd gazed at her husband, while tears rose to her eyes. "Theodore," she said, huskily, "you have realized one of my dearest hopes. With all your faults, you have always been far ahead of other men, and now — now I am almost afraid you are too perfect; you 're sure that you *do* feel quite well, and have n't any sharp pain darting through your chest?"

The following morning Mr. Hurd began to carry out his good resolutions immediately after break-fast; and when the younger children urged him to go for a walk, he informed them that "father had some very important work to do, but that they might watch him if they liked."

Mrs. Hurd met him soon afterwards mounting the attic stairs, followed by a procession of willing helpers. "Where are you going, Theodore?" she inquired.

"It is a long time since we had the tank cleaned out," he responded, "and I see no need of paying an incompetent and expensive plumber, who brings another man to stand around and look at him, for doing a simple thing like that."

"Very well, dear," his wife said, encouragingly, "only are you sure that you understand all about it?"

"Of course I do," he replied, a trifle indignantly, and Mrs. Hurd, realizing that she ought to have more confidence in him than to suggest such a possibility, retired meekly to her own room, where she quietly settled herself to her embroidery. "It is such a comfort to have Theodore interested in these little household matters," she murmured, contentedly.

"It is an education for the children, too," she meditated, as she listened to them running up and down stairs to bring their father first one thing and then another, and heard his voice from above instructing them to start all the faucets running in the bathroom, and to bring him a pail and two or three sponges.

In the course of five minutes her youngest son appeared at her elbow. "What is it, Johnnie?" she questioned.

"Father wants his other pair of glasses," he announced; "he's just smashed his best ones."

"What, those beautiful new pebbles!" Mrs. Hurd cried, regretfully; "how did it happen?"

"Oh, he was just looking down into the tank, and

they dropped off and struck on a piece of lead pipe," Johnny answered, skipping gayly away with the other pair of glasses. To him these little casualties added greatly to the enjoyment of the occasion.

In a short space of time, a rap at Mrs. Hurd's door caused her to look up from her work. In the doorway stood the cook, apparently much agitated. "Oh, mum," she gasped, breathlessly, "somethin's a leakin'! Will yez come down to the kitchen? Sure an' the ceilin's all wet and drippin' down on me."

Mrs. Hurd sprang up. "They must have let the bath-tub overflow," she exclaimed. "Come, we must all turn to with mops, cloths, and all the sponges we can get hold of."

"I suppose you know, Theodore, that you have flooded the house," she called up-stairs, adding, "Quick, Johnny, bring me down all those sponges this very minute."

As Johnny came leisurely down-stairs with the necessary sponges, he remarked, gleefully, "Pa couldn't clean it out much of any, after all; he says that no one but the plumber can get at it." At this point, having reached his mother's side, he whispered: "He's broken his other glasses, too, but he said we needn't say anything to you about it."

A little later in the morning, when the house-

hold had once more resumed its usual atmosphere
of tranquillity, Mr. Hurd entered the sitting-room
with an air of quiet determination. "I am going
to adjust that new gas-burner, that I bought so
long ago," he remarked, displaying it.

"Oh, Theodore, don't you think you had better
leave it till the gas man comes?" his wife remonstrated.

"Nonsense," he responded, "I should hope that
I could screw on a simple fixture like that. Boys,"
he added, "just run down cellar and bring me up
the tallest steps, and then ask Jane if she knows
where that monkey-wrench was put."

Mrs. Hurd withdrew once more to the seclusion
of her own apartments, after a timid protest regarding the danger of allowing the gas to escape too
freely. She embroidered peacefully for a few
moments, and was beginning to congratulate herself that all was well, when a dull thud, accompanied
by a crash, caused her to spring to her feet.

"Oh, what has happened?" she called out, in
agonized tones. "Are you killed, Theodore?"

Mrs. Hurd rushed frantically down-stairs in time
to catch sight of her husband picking himself up
from the floor where he had apparently been seated
amidst shattered fragments of several glass globes
which had accompanied his sudden descent, while
the voices of the children questioned, anxiously,
"Have you hurt yourself, papa?"

Before his family could ascertain how badly he had been injured, he rose majestically, swelling with righteous indignation, and even refusing to · allow Mrs. Hurd to examine the cut on his left wrist, which was bleeding freely from too close a contact with one of the defunct gas-globes.

"It is shameful to keep a pair of steps like that in the cellar of any respectable house," he thundered, crunching the broken glass under foot. "They are only fit for kindling wood! They should have been chopped up long ago, long ago! I never in my life saw such a shiftless set of people. Nobody takes a bit of interest in anything about the house, but everything is left for me to attend to, and I — I have nothing more important to do than to spend my time regulating the contents of the attic and the cellar, and now look at that!" and he pointed upwards to the half-adjusted gas-fixture. Mrs. Hurd turned her eyes in that direction and allowed them to rest regretfully on the chandelier, which was bent far out from its usual position and no longer hung at right angles from the ceiling.

"Never mind that, Theodore," she said, consolingly, "I 'm thankful that it broke your fall ; we shall have to get the gas man here to fix it, and he can finish adjusting the new burner at the same time, so please say you won't attempt to do anything more to it just now, won't you, Theodore ?" And Mr. Hurd said he would n't.

After luncheon, Mrs. Hurd urged that it would be a good chance for them to make a long-talked-of call on their new neighbors across the way.

"I've been waiting for you to go with me, Theodore," she ventured, persuasively, but he shook his head and insisted that he didn't feel like making calls.

"Then I'll run over without you," she said, resignedly, thinking that he might be feeling somewhat lame after his fall from "the tallest steps."

"I sha'n't be gone long," she said, pleasantly, looking into the library, where her husband was settled comfortably with his pipe and one of the magazines. "Why don't you take a nap while I'm gone?" she suggested, pausing, with her hand on the front door-knob; then she went cheerfully on her way.

When Mrs. Hurd returned, three-quarters of an hour later, a strong odor of paint greeted her nostrils, mingled with another unmistakably like benzine. "Johnny," she inquired of her youngest boy, who was buried in a book in a distant corner of the library, "where is your father?"

"Oh, he's up-stairs, painting the back entry," he responded. "I was helping him, but I got some paint on me and he sent me down here."

"On *you*," his mother exclaimed, scrutinizing him hastily, "say, rather, all over your lovely new suit. Oh, Johnny! how could you be so careless!"

Mrs. Hurd hurried up-stairs, guided by an increasing odor of paint, which plainly bespoke the continuance of Mr. Hurd's good resolutions. As she opened the door into the back entry, her husband's voice called to her to "Look out for paint! I 've painted the door on both sides," he concluded; but this warning came too late, for already her velvet cape had swept against the newly coated surface.

This was more than flesh and blood could withstand, and Mrs. Hurd's pent-up indignation burst forth.

"I should think that you had done enough harm for one day, Theodore," she exclaimed, reproachfully; "my best cape is entirely ruined, and you know it is n't paid for yet! I meant to have told you that the bill for it came only yesterday."

"Go back, don't come out here, my dear," Mr. Hurd cried excitedly, "we 've just met with an accident; they will happen in the best regulated families, you know." Here his voice took on a more persuasive tone, as he cast a hurried look at his wife, who stood like some avenging spirit in the doorway, and then he stooped down and continued to rub the carpet energetically with a roll of cloth which he held in one hand.

"Have you decided to paint the entry carpet with a whole roll of my emergency bandages, Theodore?" Mrs. Hurd said, coldly. "I thought you had bought yourself a new brush for that purpose." Then she relented slightly at sight of his dejected countenance, as he knelt upon the floor. "What was the catastrophe this time?" she questioned, mournfully.

"I was opening that largest pot of paint, and very excellent paint it is, too," he responded volubly, "when Johnny knocked my elbow, wholly by accident, my dear, and sent the contents all over the floor; so we have had rather bad work here with it, but it's pretty much all up, now," he announced, with an effort at great cheerfulness, as he gave a final rub with the emergency bandage.

"After all, this carpet is about worn out," Mr. Hurd went on, "so a little paint on it does n't matter; moreover, I told the boys that they might as well begin to take it right up, and I would see about getting a new one to-morrow. They're workers, I can tell you! Why, they have taken out all the tacks already; and, by the way, Johnny stepped on one and ran it into his foot, and I told him he had better let you look at the place, to see if there was any danger of his having lockjaw, or anything of that sort."

"I will go and bathe his foot in hot water at once," she replied, turning to depart. Then she paused and looked across the back entry at her husband, who stood confronting her in his shirt-sleeves. "May I ask why the stopper is out of that bottle of benzine?" she queried.

"Oh," he answered, meekly, putting in the cork,

" I got a little paint on my own coat, and I thought that benzine would take it off. I 've heard you say that it was the best thing — "

Mrs. Hurd lifted her skirts gingerly, and stepped across the entry carpet. " I will take your coat and get off the paint, Theodore," she said, reassuringly, " if you will promise me one thing : promise me that you will, under no circumstances, help any more about the house."

" Very well," he assented, " then I won't melt up any of that glue I brought home to mend the chairs with."

" No, no, indeed," she protested, earnestly ; " if you have any love for me, Theodore, say that you will do nothing of the sort. It is all very well for ordinary men, men who have n't your talents and ability, to do such things, but with you it is quite different ; you are capable of something better. Spend your holidays any way you like. Go to the club, go fishing, eat, smoke, play billiards, but give me your word that, whatever happens, you will never be helpful about the house again ! "

And, with his hand upon the benzine bottle, Mr. Hurd took a solemn oath that he never would.

# THE EVOLUTION OF A
BONNET

# THE EVOLUTION OF A BONNET

MISS ELIZABETH MOORE was quite a philosopher in her way, though no one would have been more astonished than she to have been told so. In fact, I doubt if her ideas about philosophers were at all distinct. Had you insisted upon a definition, she would have told you that Thornbridge, being a busy place, had no use for a class of individuals who talked instead of working, and who spent their time in thinking about things instead of buckling down and doing them.

Thornbridge was a town in which the spirit of work reigned supreme, and the thrifty inhabitants had very few idle moments in which to grow unhappy or discontented; they lived in an ideal and Arcadian atmosphere, which was as yet unspoiled by any current from the great sea of manufacturing interests. The beauty of the country was, however, beginning to attract a rapidly increasing summer population to the picturesque old town, who, with their fancy cottages and wonderful equipages, filled the sturdy inhabitants with a kind of awe, which soon gave place to a hearty dislike, as the invaders increased in numbers, and, without saying by your leave, proceeded to erect casinos and bowling-alleys and numberless other things for their own benefit, into which the worthy natives received no invitation to enter.    Moreover, the knowledge of the fact that the land obtained from the honest farmers for a mere song was sold again to others for five and six times the original amount aroused their righteous indignation, which was not lessened by the visitations of cruel and sweetly smiling ladies, who, on some pretense or other, found their way into the neat cottages and farmhouses, and who, by virtue of a few fair words and a surprisingly few silver coins, carried off old clocks, old spinning-wheels, and old china from the simple farmers' wives and daughters, to whom a little ready money seemed so much more precious than the few household treasures which they gave in return.

The substantial old farmhouse occupied by Miss Elizabeth Moore and her niece, Delight, was on the very outskirts of the village, and stood alone upon a little breezy promontory commanding a charming view of the village below.    The house and several acres of land had been Elizabeth's share of old Farmer Moore's property after his death, and in vain had been the offers of the relentless summer boarders who would have liked to build upon this desirable spot.

Miss Elizabeth was firm on these occasions, though firmness was by no means one of her ruling characteristics; she was, as her niece Delight often said, much too impulsive, and had not her niece been on hand to see that she remained unfaltering in her resolutions at some such time, it is just possible that Miss Elizabeth might, dazzled by the offer of so much money, have sold the house and land, and realized what seemed to her an enormous fortune by the transaction.

At the time of which I speak it was a perfect summer evening, with just the faintest breeze rustling through the honeysuckles on the porch. Miss Elizabeth sat stiffly in her high-backed rocker, with her knitting in her hands, and her busy needles clicked regardless of the fast-settling darkness, for she always thought with scorn of those who had to " look on " to knit.

Delight, quite unconscious of the graceful picture she made, was seated upon the upper step, with her head resting against one of the posts, about which the honeysuckle twined, forming a leafy background with its swaying tendrils and tassels, and contrasting charmingly with the wavy brown locks, which remained unruffled by the breeze. Her fine dark eyes were fixed with an intensely thoughtful expression upon a distant hill, and her hands were clasped in her lap with a firmness which denoted a mind bent upon solving some important problem.

"No, Aunt Lizzie," she was saying, "we cannot spare one cent to spend on a bonnet for me. You know that the eggs did not bring in what we expected, and it will take the last of my school money to pay for the flour on Saturday."

"Sakes alive!" exclaimed Miss Elizabeth, "I guess that man can afford to wait awhile for his money. His daughter's not in need of a bonnet, judging by what I saw of combined tail-feathers and flower-gardens on her head last Sunday. And as for ribbons, why, she must have bought the stores out. You must get you one with that kind of a high crown, Delight," she added.

"Perhaps I may, after the term is over," replied her niece, in a decided tone, which did not prevent Miss Elizabeth from entering a final protest.

"The term over, indeed!" she exclaimed, indignantly; "and the longest terms and the smallest pay! I declare it makes me provoked to think of your teaching those aggravating little boys day in and day out for an independence, and then not getting yourself a bonnet even. It was only Tuesday week when Deacon Jones told me that there was n't a girl in the village with your ability — that 's what he said — and everybody with eyes knows that there 's not one that can hold a candle to you in looks, if you 're not so stout and robust as Matilda Robinson. If it was n't for the opening of the fair I would n't feel so bad, but to see all the fine summer people in that old faded white thing, with the ribbon worse than none, why —"

"I've thought how I can fix it up very nicely, Aunt Lizzie," interrupted the girl. "And, after all, what's a bonnet? A bonnet is not everything."

"What's a bonnet!" repeated Miss Elizabeth. "A bonnet *is* everything. Don't interrupt me. I have n't lived in Thornbridge almost half a century to have my experience go for nothing. A first-class stylish bonnet or hat on a woman's head is the next best thing to a crown of glory. No man ever yet realized the importance of a bonnet. A man wears a hat to keep his head warm or cool, or to shade his eyes, and he has n't intelligence enough to know that a woman does not do the same. What sensible woman ever bought a bonnet just because it was warm, or cool, or shady? What she wants is to have it become her, and if she is once satisfied that it really does, she 'll find, and her friends 'll find, that she will wear that bonnet, and that heat and cold, or light and shade, are n't the consideration. And so," concluded Miss Elizabeth, after pausing for breath, "you just remember that the bonnet is first as well as topmost. Get on a first-class bonnet, and whether you are in Thornbridge, or sailing up the aisle of St. Peter's in Rome, you can look the whole world in the face and wear just whatever kind of dress you like."

Delight listened with great enjoyment to her aunt's earnest discourse; but all Miss Elizabeth's eloquence failed to alter her niece's determination, and the following morning saw her depart for school, taking with her the necessary money to pay for their last barrel of flour.

"And nothing left for bonnets," mused her aunt, in a tone of resignation, as she watched Delight's trim figure disappear down the road, wearing the neat but well-worn black gown, which had been made over and turned until even Delight's ingenuity had reached its limit.

After finishing the morning's work, which Miss Elizabeth never allowed to be a long process, she put on her sun-bonnet, and, trowel in hand, stepped out into the garden to spend an hour among her flowers, for the garden was her chief pride and joy. She had gone only a few steps when she became aware that a light wagonette was stopping at the gate, and a handsome, athletic young fellow, who had reined up a pair of spirited grays, jumped lightly to the ground, and helped two elegantly dressed ladies to alight. He remained, inspecting the horses, while they advanced up the path toward Miss Elizabeth, who at once put them down on the list of would-be purchasers of her land, and prepared to meet them with a dignity and firmness which should do credit to Delight's admonitions.

So she held her trowel still in hand, and bowed

stiffly from the depths of her sun-bonnet in return to their cordial salutation.

Young Mrs. Boylston, the elder of the two visitors, did most of the talking. "This is Miss Moore, I believe," she began, condescendingly; "at least they told me at the post-office that Miss Moore lived here."

"Yes, I am Miss Moore," responded Miss Elizabeth, shortly.

"You certainly have a most charming view here, and the location is perfect. I suppose the view of the village is even prettier from the piazza," Mrs. Boylston suggested.

Miss Elizabeth remained immovably in the path. "Yes," she said, dryly, "it is somewhat; but," she added briefly, "it's no use for you to look at it, for the place is not for sale, not one square inch of it."

The ladies seemed much amused at this, and Mrs. Boylston hastened to explain that they did not care to buy any land. "I have all the land I can manage now, Miss Moore, and my sister and I are merely driving about the country to find from which of the high points the view is prettiest, and," she added, sweetly, "we thought that perhaps you would ask us up on your fine breezy piazza for a moment."

Miss Elizabeth thawed at once, and endeavored to atone for her previous incivility by bringing the most comfortable chairs for them to rest upon, and begging that they would make themselves at home and stay as long as they chose. "I would ask you in," she added, "but I know it's nicer out here in the breeze."

"We should like to take a peep at your house if you're willing," both the ladies exclaimed, and Miss Elizabeth led the way into the cosy sitting-room, which they inspected with apparent interest. "I see you have one of those old clocks, Miss Moore," remarked the younger lady, advancing towards the tall timepiece in the corner. "I don't suppose you care much for an old clock like this. I would rather like to take one back to remember Thornbridge by. Don't you want to sell it to me?"

Miss Elizabeth bridled up at once. "No, I don't think of putting up my things at auction just yet; and as for relics, you will have to look for them somewhere else. Moreover, a clock that's in first-class condition, and keeps the best of time, is not much of a relic to my mind, if it is old."

The visitors, beginning to realize that they would hardly reap the desired harvest here, prepared to withdraw, after thanking Miss Moore for her kindness. Mrs. Boylston, however, whose eyes rested lovingly upon the heavy brass candlesticks, determined to make one final effort in that direction.

"I wish I knew where I could buy some candlesticks," she exclaimed. "We have such trouble getting our rooms lighted up here, where there is no gas. I don't care for very nice ones; almost anything would do, such as those, for instance," pointing to the ones on the mantel. "Of course I know that you would not part with those," she hastily added, seeing Miss Moore preparing to bridle, "but if you could tell me where to go —" As she spoke, Mrs. Boylston glanced into the mirror over the fireplace and straightened her bonnet, and at that moment Miss Elizabeth's mood changed like a flash. She would sell the old brass candlesticks; she did not care for them, and she did n't believe Delight did; and there would be some money for the new bonnet.

She surprised the ladies by remarking, "Well, I don't know as I care so much for the candlesticks, but it is quite against my principles to sell things. Still, just to oblige you, I might be willing to part with them."

Mrs. Boylston's eyes brightened with pleasure, but she only said, in a careless tone: "It would save me a good deal of trouble if you will let me have them. I will give you fifty cents for the pair."

"Very well, you may have them," said Miss Elizabeth, stiffly, already regretting that she had not shown them the door instead of humiliating herself to this extent. She had thought that the candlesticks would be worth more; but she was no judge of their value, and fifty cents would hardly buy Delight the sort of new bonnet she desired. She stepped into the china closet to get a piece of paper in which to wrap up the candlesticks, when, looking around, she saw that her visitors had followed, and were remarking that her old blue china just matched some that they had. Would n't she sell those two platters and the blue and white bowl? She would give a dollar for each platter and fifty cents for the bowl. Miss Elizabeth prepared to be indignant and to reject this offer with scorn, but instead — how she happened to do so she could not have told, except that the idea of that bonnet obliterated all others — she found herself in possession of three crisp dollar bills, and through the window she caught sight of the handsome young man stowing something under the seat, while the ladies talked and laughed in an animated way that grated terribly upon her ears.

Somehow she could not seem to settle down again to her work. She took up the trowel and tried gardening, but only for a few moments, then she came indoors again and sat down in her high-backed chair and rocked; sat there absolutely idle, if one whose thoughts are so active can be termed idle. And the more she thought, the more she became convinced that Delight would not be pleased with the transaction. Then she decided not to tell her where the money had come from until some time after the bonnet had been purchased.

Delight came home that afternoon in unusual spirits, and Miss Elizabeth watched at the doorway with pride and satisfaction as she approached with glowing cheeks and parted lips, which disclosed two rows of the whitest little teeth.

"Visitors at school to-day, Aunt Lizzie," she began, seating herself upon the steps, "and such interesting ones, too. None of your old fogies who insist upon making the boys recite something that they don't know."

"Tell me all about it, dearie," said her aunt, settling down with her knitting, and beginning to wonder how she should ever bring in the money for the bonnet successfully.

"Well, you see, auntie, they arrived just a few minutes before recess, with dear old Judge Felton, who always has been so kind to me; two beautifully dressed ladies, and, oh, such a very handsome young man! The judge introduced them as Mrs. Boylston, her sister, Miss Hollis, and her brother-in-law, Mr. Harold Boylston. Judge Felton made some embarrassing remarks about my being his pet school-marm, and I realized how very shabby my old black dress looked; but they were most agreeable, and staid and talked to me all through recess, after which they drove off in a very stylish wagon-

ette.   Mr. Boylston seemed very much interested
in my method of teaching the boys, and said he
should like to come up again some day, if I was
willing."

" How very nice of him !" remarked Miss Elizabeth, dryly.

"Yes," continued her niece, "and the Boylstons
are the people who have built that lovely new house
at the other end of the village, where we saw the
tennis-courts being marked out."

Miss Elizabeth did not broach the bonnet question that evening, but decided to wait until a more
favorable moment arrived.

The following afternoon she sat down with her
knitting to await her niece's return, and she had
just begun to wonder if Delight were not later than
usual, when she heard voices, and one of them was
distinctly masculine.   As they reached the gate, she
recognized the same young man who had driven the
spirited grays, and he carried her niece's books with
the same careless ease that had characterized his
management of the horses.   He lifted his hat and
departed, and Delight smilingly approached her
aunt.   "That was Mr. Boylston," she remarked.

" He is evidently very much interested in your
method of teaching," Miss Elizabeth said, a little
impatiently.

"Yes, he really is very much interested in the
school work, and he says that he thinks of teaching

for a couple of terms, just for the practise, now that he has finished college."

"Oh!" said her aunt, doubtfully. Then she continued, "Do you realize that it is only three days before the fair, and you have n't done a thing about that bonnet?"

"So it is," replied Delight, gravely, preparing to concentrate her whole mind upon this vital subject; "but I had a bright idea to-day while the boys were doing mental arithmetic, and I 'm sure you 'll think my new bonnet a success when you see it, and not a cent of expense, either."

"No, dear; you are to have a brand-new, stylish bonnet, and it shall cost something; and here is the money for it," she added, drawing the three bills triumphantly out of her pocket.

"Why, Aunt Lizzie, where did that come from?" cried her niece, in surprise.

"Never mind; the fairies are around sometimes, and why not here as well as elsewhere?"

But no, Delight would not be satisfied. She would not use the money till she knew where it came from, and, little by little, she drew the truth from her unwilling aunt. And then it was that Miss Elizabeth began to realize what a very dreadful thing she had done. How could she for an instant suppose that Delight would use a cent of such money? How could she have tolerated even the slightest suggestion of such a transaction? Had n't

she a particle of pride left? Oh, it was too humiliating! and Delight burst into tears. Miss Elizabeth was in the depths of despair; she had thought
that she was doing it for the best, but she saw now
that it was a great mistake. She would send the
money back, however; take it back herself, if necessary; anything, if Delight would only not feel so
badly.

Here her niece's indignation against Mrs. Boylston broke forth: "To think of entering people's
houses on false pretenses, for the purpose of cheating them out of a few things which they did not
know the value of. Three dollars, indeed! And
that young Mr. Boylston was with them at the time;
and then he dared to walk home with me after that
— up to the very gate! Interested in school-teach-
ing! I presume he wishes to have as much fun
out of the natives in his way as his sister-in-law
does in hers; but he will find that his amusement
has ceased where I am concerned."

There was to be no school on the following day,
but Delight came down earlier than usual, and Miss
Elizabeth timidly watched her determined expression and decided step as she moved about the
house, seemingly unconscious of her aunt's strenu-
ous efforts to atone for her unpardonable offense
by preparing as many of her favorite dishes as possible. Delight, however, exhibited but very little
appetite for breakfast, but noticing the expression

of deep gloom settling over her aunt's face when she had twice refused to taste the delicately browned waffles, she impulsively threw her arms about Miss Elizabeth's neck, and, kissing her, exclaimed:

"Don't you worry a bit more about anything, auntie. I am the most ungrateful girl living, and you are the sweetest and most unselfish creature in the whole world. I will make things all right, and you shall see me in a bonnet which you shall be proud of."

The breakfast dishes cleared away, Delight set to work at once upon the old and well-worn bonnet. It was a light straw, trimmed with buff ribbons, which had long since faded into a doubtful white. The straw was still in very good condition, although the shape was sadly out of style. Miss Elizabeth eyed it mournfully, but Delight set to work with an amount of assurance which could not but inspire the most skeptical with confidence. She soaked the old straw thoroughly in water, and then, taking possession of the brown bread mould, shaped the crown skilfully over its top, and, after bending the brim of the bonnet up at just the proper angle, fastened it firmly in place by winding string about it and left it to dry. "That shape will be just the latest agony," she announced to Miss Elizabeth. "And now for my ribbon. I'm going to dye it cardinal."

She produced a small package of red powder,

and, after dissolving it in water, plunged in all the faded buff ribbon, which came forth a beautiful shade of dark red; and, when it was ironed out, even Miss Elizabeth acknowledged that it could hardly have been told from new. "Though it is perhaps a trifle stiff," she added.

"Do you suppose that those old pink roses would take the color, too?" questioned Delight, a moment later.

To which her aunt replied, "We can see," and brought them down forthwith.

Delight let them sink deep into the red liquid, and then drew them carefully out, and hung them to dry near the stove. They really looked remarkably well.

By this time the straw was dry and pressed firmly into shape, and it now only remained to be trimmed. Here Delight showed herself mistress of her art, for her bows never flopped down when they should have stood up, nor stuck out where they should have gone in, and she caught up the red roses on one side in just the most becoming way, showing enough to let you know that they were red roses, and yet not too much, to thrust upon your consciousness the fact that they were not perhaps the most perfect kind of roses.

At last it was finished, and the successful artist tied the bow under her chin, and stood before the old-fashioned mirror inspecting her morning's work.

" It is perfectly lovely," Miss Elizabeth declared, with enthusiasm, "and I should think it had come straight from Paris."

After dinner Delight arrayed herself in her best gown (it was a pale gray cashmere, and perfectly simple, but it fitted her graceful figure without a wrinkle), and then, after adjusting the new bonnet, which still filled her aunt with awe and admiration, she drew on her silk gloves, and prepared to start out.

Miss Elizabeth did not dare to ask any questions with regard to her mission, but she did venture to call after her in a frightened tone, " Don't do anything that you may be sorry for, Delight."

" No, Aunt Lizzie," she returned, in a calm voice, as she moved slowly down the walk, stopping only long enough to put one dark-red rose into her buttonhole.

A little later in the afternoon Mrs. Boylston was languidly reclining in a hammock on the airy upper veranda which overlooked the wide lawn, where her sister and young Mr. Boylston had been engaged in a game of tennis, for which, however, they seemed to feel very little enthusiasm, as they had returned to the upper piazza. Miss Hollis had dropped into a steamer chair, and young Boylston was sitting upon the balustrade deeply intent upon trying to balance his racquet upon one finger. At this moment a servant appeared, bringing word that Miss Moore would like to see Mrs. Boylston.

"Miss Moore?" queried the lady. "Who can she be? Well, ask her to come up here. Why, she must be the woman who sold me the candlesticks and those fascinating platters," she continued. "I saw a platter like them in town not long ago, and the man at the shop asked me seven dollars for it, and I got mine for a dollar apiece, Harold."

"By George!" exclaimed her brother-in-law, jumping up, "I call that a most shameful business, cheating country people out of their few household gods? To my mind, it's the smallest kind of swindling when the rich cheat the poor, and I should n't think you would be overproud of the transaction."

The conversation was suddenly arrested by the arrival of Miss Moore upon the scene. It was a trying ordeal for her, but she boldly faced the enemy's guns, and, with sparkling eyes and head erect, advanced without flinching. Both the ladies rose, and greeted her with a cool friendliness which hardly disguised their evident surprise at receiving a call from the pretty schoolmistress. Harold Boylston's pleasure was quite evident, and he brought forward a large arm-chair, saying, "Won't you sit here, Miss Moore?"

But Delight remained standing. "I wished to see you only for a moment, Mrs. Boylston," she began, in a clear voice, "to return some money which my aunt received from you the other day.

We are not in the habit of parting with our household possessions, which we value rather for their family associations than for their actual worth, which you doubtless appreciate better than we." Mrs. Boylston winced. "Pray accept the platters and the candlesticks," she continued, "if they please you, as it is a great pleasure for simple country people like ourselves to contribute in any way toward the happiness or amusement" (here her eyes rested coldly upon Harold) "of those who, like yourself, can so easily gratify every wish. We are only too glad to give them to you, Mrs. Boylston. Good afternoon," and, thrusting the three dollars into that offended lady's hand, Miss Moore swept from the piazza with the scornful air of a princess.

"Isn't she just superb?" exclaimed young Boylston, warmly. "She crushed you completely, Nelly, and — "

"To think of an ignorant country girl like that daring to confront me with such impudence!" cried Mrs. Boylston, angrily.

"You didn't get half you deserved," rejoined Harold, swinging himself over the railing, with asperity. I wish she had told you what she really thought of you. If that is your idea of an ignorant country girl, it's not mine; and as for style, why, there was an atmosphere about that bonnet which few of your New Yorkers could rival. I'm off for a constitutional, ladies, so you can fight it out between you."

As he disappeared across the lawn, Mrs. Boylston sank back into her hammock with a sigh. " I do so hate scenes," she murmured; "and Harold of late seems to take pleasure in saying unkind, cutting things to me. I 'm sure I have never objected to his flirting with any number of country girls, and I don't know why he should be so ugly about a few old candlesticks. But I shall have those things sent right back this very evening. After that girl's absurd conduct, I would not have them in the house another night."

Meanwhile Delight was walking briskly along the shady lane. She felt that she had passed through the trying ordeal with success; perhaps her display of pride and spirit had made her appear ridiculous, and even now they were probably laughing at her; but she did not care. They might laugh on the surface, but they knew down in their hearts that she had had the best of the encounter; and Mr. Boylston had really looked quite as if he thought so, too. How becoming a tennis suit was to him !

Just at this point she arrived at the cross-roads, where, much to her amazement, she encountered that very individual turning the corner with a calm and unruffled demeanor, which told no tales of his brisk run across the fields. Delight, however, re-

sented his assured air, and showed none of the surprise which she felt at his sudden appearance, but
regarded him with perfect indifference.

"Are you provoked with me, too?" he inquired,
in an injured tone. "I declare, I am so afraid of
you that the power of speech has quite deserted me
after the magnificent way in which you sailed into
Mrs. Boylston just now. I'm not sure that you will
have anything to say to me, though I can't see why
I am responsible for people who are only my connections by marriage. Please may I walk home
with you, Miss Moore?"

Delight, who had determined upon her course of
action, replied ironically that she was glad to see
that fright had not robbed him of the use of his
legs as well as of his tongue, but that it would be
quite unnecessary for him to go any farther in that
direction.

"I am glad of that," he responded, gayly. "I
hate to do necessary things, and I know you do,
only you won't acknowledge it. When I walk with
a pretty girl I do it not because it is necessary, but
because it is agreeable."

"Agreeable to whom?" interrupted Delight.

"To both of us," replied Boylston, looking into
her eyes with one of his most irresistible glances.

"Speak for yourself," replied his companion,
coolly.

"That's a very dangerous remark to make to any

impetuous young fellow," responded he, meditatively; "it played the dickens with poor John Alden, you know, and left Miles Standish disconsolate."

"It is certainly a rather superfluous remark to make to you, Mr. Boylston," said Delight, who found it most difficult to remain stern and unbending.

Boylston decided to try a different tack, so he stopped suddenly, and lifting his hat said, gravely: "If my company is really distasteful to you, Miss Moore, I will not thrust it upon you any longer, but will bid you good-afternoon."

"Good-afternoon," responded Delight, sweetly, continuing to walk rapidly away from him, and without a glance in his direction.

This was not satisfactory, however, and Harold Boylston started at once after the departing figure. "On second thoughts," he said, reaching her side, "I think I won't say good-afternoon just yet."

"Second thoughts are not always the best," replied Delight, greeting his sudden reappearance with perfect indifference.

"I don't care about their being so always; it is enough satisfaction to have them best just now," said Boylston, who saw with much pleasure that a reassuring twinkle was beginning to manifest itself in his companion's eyes.

"It is no use," she laughed, "I really can't be provoked with you, you're so absurd."

"I don't know why you should be provoked with me," Boylston protested, with an air of injured innocence. "I have n't done anything worse than to tell my sister-in-law what I thought of her little bric-à-brac transactions, in not the most complimentary terms, either. Why did n't your aunt snub her, as she deserved, on the spot? I do not see how she came to let my worthy connections indulge in their favorite pastime. I 'm afraid she has not your spirit. I wish you had been there to give them a piece of your mind." There was such an unmistakable ring of sincerity in his voice that Delight could not but relent, and then, as Aunt Elizabeth must be vindicated, she told him all about the bonnet.

"It is a perfect stunner," cried Boylston, enthusiastically, regarding her with undisguised admiration.

"Only my fingers are rather pink still," said Delight, drawing off one of her silk gloves and eyeing her finger-tips ruefully. "But," she continued, "I was very cross to Aunt Elizabeth when I came home and found out what she had done. I was just horrid, but you can't think how humiliated I felt."

"Yes, I can," broke in Boylston, warmly. "I know just how you felt; you hated us all, and knew that I was just as bad as the rest, only worse."

"Yes," assented Delight, frankly, "I thought a great many unpleasant things about you, and said that I did not care to amuse the summer residents in company with old clocks and candlesticks."

"I'll renounce my claims to being a summer resident and become a native, if you'll only restore me to favor and be friends," he protested.

By the time Miss Moore's gate had been reached this request had evidently been granted, and Miss Elizabeth, who had been anxiously awaiting her niece's return, was much astonished to see her come back quite on the best of terms with that very same not-to-be-tolerated young man.

She showed no surprise, however, when Delight introduced Mr. Boylston, but invited him to come in and rest awhile after his walk, which he did without waiting for further urging, and spent a good long hour. His last words before taking leave were: "I shall be on the lookout for that lovely red bonnet at the fair to-morrow."

When he had gone, Miss Elizabeth listened with great interest to the afternoon's proceedings. At the end of the recital she drew a long sigh of relief. "But it does n't seem as though you snubbed the young man much," she finally remarked.

"I tried my best, Aunt Lizzie, but he would n't be snubbed," said Delight, thoughtfully.

That night Mrs. Boylston's man brought up a bundle addressed to Miss Moore, which, when opened, was found to contain two platters, a blue and white bowl, and a pair of brass candlesticks.

Harold Boylston had promised to escort the ladies to the agricultural fair, and they insisted upon his being in constant attendance upon them, and upon his telling them all about the horses, the cows, and the sheep. Miss Hollis made him ask first how many inches the prize squash measured, and then how much the largest bunch of grapes weighed, while Mrs. Boylston sent him to inquire if she could buy any of the prize apples afterwards, until his much-tried patience quite gave way. For, in the distance, he saw Delight's red bonnet, now pausing beside the fancy sheep, while he must needs examine squashes, and then inspecting the prize bantams, while his sister-in-law dragged him over to look at a kind of lawn-mower that would roll the grass in the most approved style. Morever, his interest in lawn-mowers was not increased by his knowledge of the fact that his own classmate, Charlie Felton, who had proved to be old Judge Felton's nephew, was by Delight's side, and acted as though he expected to remain there for the rest of the day.

He suddenly slipped away, just as Mrs. Boylston was looking at the Plymouth Rock hens, and hastened towards the fascinating red bonnet. Delight seemed very glad to see him, and Felton greeted him with evident surprise.

"Why, where did you come from, Boylston?"

"I'm so glad to see you, Charlie, and my sister

and Miss Hollis are dying to speak to you. Don't you see them over there? I'll take care of Miss Moore while you run over and say how d 'ye do."

"I should be charmed to see them again, of course," exclaimed Felton, whose countenance, however, failed to express the greatest pleasure at the immediate prospect; "but I have promised to show Miss Moore some of my uncle's prize apples first, so I'll see you a little later," and Felton prepared to move on.

His friend was not to be thus easily baffled. "I'm going to show Miss Moore the giant turnips," he persisted, "while you just speak to my sister. See, she 's is waving her parasol now."

There was nothing for Felton to do but to go, and his friend smiled with satisfaction at his reluctant departure. "Suppose we walk down to the end of the grove, where there is n't such a crowd, and where we can cool off," he suggested.

"But you were going to take me to see the giant turnips," protested Delight; "and, besides, if we go off there, Mr. Felton will never find us."

"I don't intend that he shall," was Boylston's mental comment, but he only said: "Oh, I don't think he will have any difficulty. You don't suppose that I really wanted to show you giant turnips, do you? I hate such things. It is bad enough for such unpalatable substances as turnips to exist without their having the effrontery to grow to any such unwieldy size. I was only trying to offset Felton's apples. But if you're so interested in those monstrosities, we will go up into that hot place and look at them."

As Delight expressed no great desire to do so, they strolled down through the grove which led out of the grounds, and Boylston espied an inviting rustic bench, on which they might rest in the shade of the tall pines.

Felton, meanwhile, had been cordially welcomed by Mrs. Boylston and her sister, who at once appropriated him in a manner he hardly relished. Harold had disappeared, and he saw no means of escape, so he asked the ladies to come up and look at the prize turnips, where he hoped to encounter that deceitful individual.

Harold, however, was not in the vicinity of the turnips. About this time, Mrs. Boylston casually remarked, "I wonder what has become of Harold," and Felton at once rose to the emergency.

"He is probably having hard work to find us in this crowd. Now, if you ladies will take a seat on that bench, I will look him up."

"Oh, no matter, Mr. Felton," they exclaimed, reassuringly, "don't trouble yourself about him." They were both more than satisfied with his society.

"It is no trouble at all," he hastened to assure them. "I will find him in just one moment," and he dashed off into the yard.

"What a handsome fellow he is!" commented Mrs. Boylston; "and so very obliging and energetic. Now Harold is so lazy."

"He is too obliging," Miss Hollis rejoined. "He need not have been so anxious to find Harold; it was just an excuse to get away. I don't see why you wanted to see Harold, when we have had so much of his society, and I'm sure he was grumpy enough when I asked him about those ugly little pigs with their tails all out of curl. You see if Mr. Felton comes back with Harold, that's all. What uncomfortable seats these are. I wish the man who made them had to sit in them for the rest of his life."

"There wouldn't be much rest of his life if he did," replied her sister.

"Don't," faintly murmured Miss Hollis. "How can you joke in this hot, wretched place?"

During this time, Felton, who had reached the yard, was pausing a moment to think. "I might have known Boylston would skip off and leave me for the rest of the day, but I'll get even with him on the monopolizing business. He is probably down in the grove." So saying, Felton hastened in that direction, and was soon rewarded by a glimpse of the most attractive red bonnet not far away.

"Now I call this true enjoyment," Boylston was just saying. "This is my first experience of agricultural fairs, and I think they are the best fun in the world."

At this point a most unwelcome voice interrupted.

"So this is the way you show Miss Moore prize turnips, is it? Boylston, you are a man of excellent taste."

"That's why I let the turnips alone," responded Harold.

"It is perfect up here in the shade," continued Felton, "and I'm sorry to break up your *tête-à-tête*, but your sister sent me after you, and she wants you immediately. I told her I would send you back at once. You will find her up there by those turnips you spoke of."

Harold Boylston rose reluctantly. "Suppose we all go up together to see those apples, Felton? Won't you come up, Miss Moore?"

"No; I think I will cool off a little longer," said Delight, glancing mischievously at Felton, who had dropped into Boylston's seat. "And remember that your sister is waiting for you."

Boylston strode off, leaving the field and the rustic bench in possession of his friend, who took no pains to conceal his pleasure.

Mrs. Boylston and Miss Hollis saw him approach through the crowd. "Here we have been sitting alone on this board for a perfect age," they both cried. "What have you done with Mr. Felton?"

"What did you send him after me for? Could n't you do without me for a few minutes? Felton knows a sight more about pigs and turnips than I do. I did my part hunting up an interesting man for you, and it's not my fault if you can't hold on to him for five minutes. I could n't very well chain him up for you."

"I did n't send him for you, Harold. I just said I wondered what had become of you, and off he rushed; but I supposed, of course, he would come back."

"I told you he would n't," put in her sister. "And now, Harold, please find the wagonette and drive us home. I am tired to death of animals and vegetables, and I think agricultural fairs are perfectly horrid. I have been once to see what they are like, and now that I know, I shall never come again."

Harold found the horses without a word, and drove them home in solemn silence. Mrs. Boylston was most enthusiastic about the lovely view as they drove along, but he was only conscious that he had left Felton in possession of the rustic seat and the bewitching owner of the red bonnet.

Felton had always spent his vacations with his uncle in Thornbridge, and he and Delight were old friends. This time he had only run down for two or three days, and Boylston learned with pleasure the following day that he had gone back to town.

During the weeks which followed, Boylston became what Miss Elizabeth termed "steady company." He and Delight were the best of friends,
and as her vacation had begun, he had ample chance
to indulge in ideal drives, walks, and talks. But
the best of friends must part, and the brightest days
will end, and Harold's good times were brought to
a close by a telegram from his father, which announced that his immediate presence in town was
both desirable and necessary. He had really forgotten during the last few weeks that there were
such words as time or town. Now he suddenly
realized how very pleasant it had all been, and how
he should miss Delight's dark eyes and enchanting
smile. He tried to persuade himself, however, that
it was all a fleeting summer episode. He should
not think so much about Delight when he was once
in town, and she — she would forget him, of course,
very soon. Would she? This last thought did not
give him the satisfaction that he had expected to
derive from it. He decided to take the evening
train up to the city, and in the afternoon he went
up and bade Delight and Miss Elizabeth good-by.
Delight took his announcement with a calmness
which did not please him as it should have done,
and she was provokingly silent while Miss Elizabeth
protested how much they should miss him. He had
determined to leave in the highest of spirits, in
which they were to share; but his efforts did not

seem to be crowned with success, and his jokes
failed to call forth any response from Delight's
abstracted gaze.   At last he rose to go.

"I shall look for a continuation of my good times
next summer, Miss Moore," he said, shaking hands
with Delight.

"Good-by, Mr. Boylston.   We shall always be
glad to see you," she replied, quietly, steadily returning his searching look.   And Boylston, lifting
his hat, walked rapidly down through the long rows
of hollyhocks, which he fancied closed behind him,
shutting him out from all that was best and most
beautiful.

His sister was not going back to town until the
following week.   Having packed his valise and
swallowed a hasty supper, he set out for the station,
after refusing the ladies' offer to drive him down to
the train, as he hoped that the walk would make
him feel better.   By the time he reached the station,
however, he felt much worse.   If Delight had cared
anything for him she could not have said good-by
so calmly.   Would she forget him as soon as he
had gone?   He knew that he could not forget her
for one moment, nor could he deceive himself longer
on that score.   He loved her, and always should love
her, not less as time went on, but more and more.
How unfeeling he had been to leave without a word!
He deserved her utmost scorn.

While he stood waiting for the down-train, the

train from the city came in, and he caught sight of Felton alighting with bag, fishing-tackle, and tennis-racquet. He had come down for his vacation.

"How d'ye do, Boylston?" he called out, cheerfully. "So you're off on the eight o'clock train, are you?"

Boylston's feelings underwent a sudden change. A wild jealousy took possession of him, and with it came a sudden determination. The eight o'clock train was rapidly coming into sight.

"I say, Felton," he cried, grasping him by the hand.

"What is it?" demanded Felton.

"Go up and spend the evening with my worthy relatives. I had to rush off quite suddenly, and I fancy that they are rather upset. I'll be everlastingly grateful if you'll go there to-night, Charlie."

Felton hesitated. He had meant to stroll over to the Moore's, but he would have the field there to himself, now that Boylston had gone, so he promised, and departed.

Harold entered the station, and deposited his bag in the waiting-room. When he emerged upon the platform again, the last car of the down-train was just disappearing from view.

"Lost your train, Mr. Boylston?" queried the station-master.

"Yes," he replied, calmly. "There is nothing now till the midnight train, is there?"

Delight was sitting on her favorite step, with her head resting among the honeysuckles. She had just returned from a walk to a neighbor's, where she and Miss Elizabeth had been invited to tea. She had pleaded a headache, and had come home, leaving her aunt to enjoy herself with the others.

The moon was slowly rising above the hills, but Delight was quite unconscious of the fact. Two large tears were rolling down her cheeks, as she sat there, silent and motionless. In her hand she held her red bonnet, which she had taken off; she looked at it, scornfully, and at last tossed it impatiently on to the step by her side, and buried her face in the honeysuckles.

Can Aunt Lizzie have returned so soon? She must not find her crying.

"Good-evening, Miss Moore," said an unmistakable voice.

"Why, Mr. Boylston, where did you come from?" she said, faintly, sinking back into the depths of the vines.

"From the station, to be sure. I lost the eight o'clock train, you see," he added, "so I thought I would come up and say good-by over again."

"Was the first good-by so pleasant that you wanted a repetition?" she murmured.

"No, it was not," he exclaimed, quite fiercely, sitting down on the step beside her, but he rose again, immediately. "What is this?" he cried, producing a much-flattened object.

"My bonnet," she responded, beginning to laugh.

"Oh, I'm so sorry," he said, holding it up, and regarding it ruefully. "That lovely bonnet!"

"It's no matter," laughed Delight; "for I had decided to indulge in a new one."

Boylston still held it up mournfully. "There can never be another as pretty or as interesting. You may get a very beautiful one, but you can never have another bonnet like this. I shall never feel the same toward any other bonnet. Delight," he cried, impetuously, "have you been crying? You were just a little sorry to have me go? I could not go until I had made sure of that. Dearest, I love you. Will you be my wife?" .

When Miss Elizabeth returned, later in the evening, she was more than astonished to find that the recently departed Boylston was not on his way to the city, and that Delight's headache was completely cured.

And Felton, true to his word, spent a long and quiet evening with Mrs. Boylston and her sister, after assuring them that he had left Harold just boarding the eight o'clock train. It was a great satisfaction to him to feel that his friend was safely back in town.

And Harold Boylston thought kindly of Felton as he stepped aboard the midnight train. "I never appreciated, before," he said to himself, "what a first-rate fellow Felton is."

# MRS. HUDSON'S PICNIC

# MRS. HUDSON'S PICNIC

MRS. HUDSON especially disliked picnics, and never went on them if she could possibly help doing so, but in this instance, circumstances over which, at best, she had very little control decidedly got the upper hand of her and forced her to submit gracefully.

Circumstances, in the guise of a dozen or more young people, attacked her on every side — in the breakfast-room, on the hotel piazza, and even in the seclusion of her own apartment, to which she fled in vain for refuge. Here the enemy tapped aggressively, and entered triumphantly, to seat themselves upon her trunks and continue their persuasions; they said that none of the mothers would go on a picnic up the river with them, but that she was so lovely they knew she would n't refuse; moreover, they added that all the girls in the hotel adored her, and the young men had been heard to declare that she was "perfectly fine." They concluded by saying that they would rather have her than any one else, for everything depended upon the chaperon;

there were plenty of stupid people that they could get if they wished to, but they wanted somebody bright and interesting, like herself.

When Mrs. Hudson crossed the parlor, two or three sweet young girls twined their arms about her, and if she stepped into the office for a moment, a couple of young fellows joined her and hung upon her casual remarks with breathless interest.

In short, there was nothing for a kind-hearted woman to do but to consent to chaperon such appreciative young people.

"Mother says that she would have gone if she were not so timid in a boat," one of the girls announced; and "Aunt Mary is afraid of the river in the evening, on account of her sensitive throat," put in another; "we're so glad that you're not one of the delicate kind, Mrs. Hudson."

Mrs. Hudson smiled faintly. She was miserably timid in a boat herself, and also wretchedly sensitive to the dampness of the river, but she made up her mind that even an attack of bronchitis would be preferable to dispelling the exalted illusions which were cherished regarding her.

The young people, having obtained her unwilling consent, at once went ahead with their preparations, after assuring her that she needn't worry about anything, unless she felt like looking after the luncheon, which was only a trifle, of course. The charge of this small detail she readily assumed, and, in conse-

quence, brought down upon herself the wrath of
the not too obliging proprietor, who overheard her
speaking about it to the head waiter, and availed
himself of the occasion to announce that he was
tired of this lunch business, that he had had enough
of it, and that he had already told the young people
so, two weeks ago.

These and other similar remarks made the prospective chaperon wish that she had undertaken
to superintend any other detail than this, despite
its triviality. She discovered soon, however, that
there was a still more serious phase attendant upon
the getting up of a small picnic. If it had been a
big picnic, everybody would at least have had an invitation ; but being a small one, only a select few could
be so favored. And the pioneers went ahead and
asked whom they chose, and then screened themselves behind the fact that it was " Mrs. Hudson's
picnic." It was useless for her to assure the indignant relatives and supporters of those not asked
that she had nothing to do with it, for they did not
believe her, and the result was averted glances, when
she entered the dining-room, in place of the usual
friendly greetings.

The morning dawned in cloudy uncertainty,
which is by far the most aggravating thing a picnic day can do. Mrs. Hudson ventured feebly that
it looked like rain, but was at once overruled and
convinced that the day would be all the finer for a

cloudy beginning, and that they might feel sure of
superb moonlight to come home by.

About noontime the sun peeped cautiously out for
a half-hour, and, by so doing, confirmed everybody
in the belief that it had cleared off gloriously.

With a deep sigh, born of desperate determination,
Mrs. Hudson stepped unsteadily from the boat landing on to the gunwale of the boat which was waiting
to receive the chaperon, and nearly capsized it at
the start.

" I asked you not to step on the gunwale, Mrs.
Hudson," exclaimed the young man who was assist-
ing her, with as much politeness as he could sum-
mon after fishing up his coat and one of the cushions, which had been jerked overboard.

" Yes, I heard you," gasped Mrs. Hudson, humbly;
" but I didn't know what the gunwale was; if you
had said you meant the edge I should have been
more careful."

Five other boats and one canoe were needed to
contain the entire party, and finally, after much dis-
cussion and changing about, the picnickers were
found to be actually "all aboard."

Mrs. Hudson having discovered what the gunwale
was, grasped it firmly with both hands as she sat in
the stern of the boat, and a moment later acquired
more wisdom by getting her fingers pinched against
the end of the pier as she swung about.

"Where is the luncheon?" somebody inquired

loudly. "Did n't you bring it down with you, Tom?" somebody else called out. In response to this, Tom was seen to leap ashore and disappear in the direction of the hotel.

"We'd better start ahead," some one shouted, and the other boats were promptly headed up-stream.

Mrs. Hudson leaned against the damp cushions in the stern and watched the scudding clouds a little uneasily. By the time that the "picnic pines," which were two miles up the river, came into sight, the scurrying clouds had begun to descend in pattering raindrops. Out came the mackintoshes and up went umbrellas, but every one remained cheerful. "Only a shower," several voices announced gaily.

It proved to be a very heavy one, and Mrs. Hudson tried to hold her umbrella over the oarsman nearest her; he begged her, however, to shelter instead his pet banjo, which was tucked under one of the seats. "Just keep that dry, Mrs. Hudson," he said, "and I don't care how wet I am." Mrs. Hudson took off the cape of her mackintosh and wrapped it around the banjo, and held her umbrella tenderly over it while she sat with her feet in a pool of water, and the boat grew momentarily more and more wet and slippery.

"Here we are," somebody called out, and Mrs. Hudson peered from under her umbrella, and had the satisfaction of seeing the picnic pines rising gloomy and damp before her. It was still raining, though less heavily, as the unhappy chaperon, with the precious banjo clasped to her heart, jumped heavily from the boat into eight inches of soft mud, and clambered up a steep and slippery bank, followed by the dripping picnickers.

"Don't any of you think of sitting down unless you wish to have pneumonia," she exclaimed, warningly, as she stood under a sheltering tree and peeped at the banjo to see if it was injured.

"This won't last long," several voices assured her; "it's beginning to break away already," and sure enough, a bit of blue sky was really visible, and a moment later the drops ceased to fall.  Mrs. Hudson picked her way over the wet pine-needles and murmured, "I hope it will dry off a little before we have our supper."

"Where is that other boat with the supper in it?" one of the young men inquired, and everybody now looked anxiously down the river for it, but no boat was in sight.

"It's great fun to be up here in the wet without any supper," one or two began to grumble.

"I don't believe they'll come at all, now," another said gloomily; "they probably put back when it began to rain."

"And took it for granted that we would do the same," concluded a third, mournfully.

"Perhaps we had better go back, then," Mrs. Hudson suggested timidly, casting a longing glance toward the boats, but nobody seconded her motion, and the young people began to explore the grove or seated themselves on the rocks near the water to watch for the missing boat.

The chaperon spread her mackintosh upon a board and sat patiently down upon it. She tried to be bright and cheerful, and thought up all the jokes and conundrums that still lingered in her memory, and even told one or two funny stories, a most unusual feat for her.

In the course of half an hour a welcome speck "hove into sight," and all set up a grateful shout, "The supper! It has come at last." And a few minutes later the delinquent Tom scrambled ashore, all unconscious of the anxiety he had occasioned, exclaiming, "I should have been here before if I had n't anchored under the bridge to wait for the shower to be over."

Seated cross-legged about a friendly rock, the picnickers joyfully passed the sandwiches around in a couple of moistened box-covers, and regaled themselves with ginger pop and hard-boiled eggs, which were not boiled as hard as they should have been.

" Now this is something like!" they cried out, as the salt, wrapped in a piece of newspaper, went from hand to hand. One of the young men knocked the head off a bottle of olives, cutting his finger in the process, and then set the bottle down beside the chocolate cake, where some one immediately tipped it over, thereby saturating the cake with brine.

This did not injure the cake any, however, as several critics tested it and declared that it was " delicious," and tasted much improved in consequence. All kept asking Mrs. Hudson if it was n't great fun, and she tried to say conscientiously that it was, though she had hardly recovered from the effects of having a bottle of ginger ale poured over her, before one of the young men, in his efforts to open a box of sardines with his knife, sent the whole of it into her lap upside down.

Mrs. Hudson shuddered as she raised her bottle of ginger ale to her lips ; she had always considered it the height of depravity to drink from a bottle. She picked up a hard cracker and bit it thoughtfully, after brushing off a stray ant which was running over it, and mentally decided that no kind-hearted impulse should ever again put her in a like position.

Supper ended, the young people, after offering to help the chaperon clear up the remains, strolled off in different directions, leaving her to restore to the empty baskets unaided, the remainder of the hotel property. As she walked to the water's edge and threw overboard the last empty bottle, she heard the voices of the young people singing snatches of popular airs, and the twang of the banjo assured her that the instrument had come ashore unscathed, thanks to her protecting mackintosh. But now, once again, the rain-drops began to patter down. Alas for any possibilities of moonlight !

" Come, we must go at once," Mrs. Hudson insisted ; " it is raining again."

The picnickers beat a hasty retreat to their boats, which were unpleasantly wet and uncomfortable by this time. The weary chaperon was handed hastily into her boat, and staggered wildly towards the stern of it, assuring those who were helping her that she was " all right," an assertion which she immediately proved to be false by tripping over a foot-rest in the darkness, and sitting down sooner than she had intended in consequence, and causing the boat to tip far to starboard.

An ominous snap sounded and she rose hastily, but, alas ! too late, exclaiming, " Oh, what have I done ? Why did you put it there ? I 've spoiled that lovely banjo ! "

Harder and faster came down the rain, as silently, and with all possible speed, the six boats and the one canoe flew homewards. Never had two miles seemed so long before to Mrs. Hudson. She sat in terrified suspense, expecting that every moment would be her last, as she was rushed along in the darkness. Once they ran aground upon a small island, and again they struck the moorings of an absent fishing craft sharply ; but at last a welcome thump told that the pier had been safely reached.

The rain fell fast and pitilessly as Mrs. Hudson

stood upon the wharf and waited the arrival of the canoe, which had fallen far astern of all the other boats.

Now as they watched for it, vague and appalling suspicions flitted through the chaperon's tired brain. Had the canoe been upset? Had the occupants been drowned? What should she say to their fond parents if that were the case? She could never return to the hotel to face their heartrending reproaches. While she was meditating upon some means of escape from such a dreadful possibility the canoe glided quietly up to the wharf, but in the anxiety that she had endured in those ten awful minutes Mrs. Hudson felt that she had added ten years to her age.

"We have had a magnificent time in spite of the showers," cried the picnickers, as they flocked into the hotel office, wet and bedraggled. Mrs. Hudson would have smiled at the word "showers" had she felt energetic enough to do so; but as it was, she only ordered hot lemonade and dragged her tired frame up-stairs.

She arose the next morning with a severe cold on her chest (which lasted for many weeks), and descended to be greeted by the reproaches of the mothers of those who went upon the picnic, because she let them stay out in the rain, and to be coldly avoided by those others who were not favored with an invitation to "her picnic," and as she sat alone and miserable in the parlor, with her chuddah shawl drawn up about her ears, these words were wafted towards her through an open window: " If we could have had a real jolly chaperon, it might have been some fun, but she is a perfect stick, and the only thing that she could do was to sit down on Harry Carter's banjo and smash it."

# A BAG OF POP-CORN

# A BAG OF POP-CORN

JEREMIAH TUFTS was packing up his things "to go home," he told his friend Sam Wilkins; though when he stopped to think the matter over, he had to own to himself that the place he was about to leave was in reality much more his home than the one for which he was bound.

· Sam had dropped in upon him, and was watching with a troubled look his preparations to leave the place he had occupied for so many years. It was hard for Sam to get over the shock which he had experienced when his friend had suddenly announced his decision to return East; and he tried in vain to reconcile Jeremiah's usual calm and stolid demeanor with his apparent feverish anxiety to be off at once. He sat on a rude chair, which Jeremiah had always considered one of his triumphs in furniture manufacture, and puffed his clay pipe. Jeremiah was nailing up in a large packing-case such of his household goods as he deemed worthy of transportation.

"I hope you 'll help yourself, Sam, to anythin'

that strikes you as available," he remarked, taking a nail out of his mouth and preparing to drive it into the case; "I sha'n't tote any of the furniture away with me," he added, reflectively. "It ain't much of anythin' to speak of, but it might come in handy, some of it."

This liberality elicited no response from Sam, who continued to regard him seriously, shaking his head. "It ain't natural and I can't say it seems right to me," he said at last.

"Why, not, I should like to know? Why ain't it right and natural to give away a lot of old things I've got no further use for?"

"You don't understand me, Jeremiah. It wa'n't the furniture I was referrin' to; it was to yourself, man. Here you've lived and worked among us quiet and contented these twenty years, and everythin' about here's seemed to suit you. I've heard you say time and ag'in that no place ever combined to satisfy you like this, and now, all of a sudden, you pack up and say you're goin' to leave us. There's somethin' extraordinarily wrong the matter with you, Jeremiah, I'm afraid, and I wish you'd let me ask the doctor to come 'round and take a look at you."

Jeremiah, having finished nailing up the packing-case, drew himself slowly up on top of it, and sat there, regarding his friend. "Don't you be a wor-ryin' about me, Sam. I wa'n't never better in my life. Moreover, I'd like to make one remark, which is, if it ain't right and natural for a man to want to go and end his days in his own native town, I want to know what is right and natural."

"Yes, if you have a home a-waitin' for you; but you've told me many a time that you hadn't a relation in the world. And you've allowed how you was pretty much a pilgrim and a stranger altogether."

Jeremiah cleared his throat. "You don't understand," he said, "it's the old associations and p'ints of interest; and," he hesitated, "I'd mighty like to look up a few of the old friends."

"If you'd been anxious about lookin' them up, I should have thought you'd have sot about it before this. Likely you'd have found more of 'em standin' around to receive you ten years ago than you will now."

A deep shade of melancholy rested upon Jeremiah's face. "I wish I had started ten years ago," he said, sadly. He was silent for a moment, and then went on: "I've been savin' up somethin', and I believe it's enough to answer for my bein' tolerably comfortable from now on, with a margin to pay for a respectable monument in the old buryin'-ground on the hill."

His friend again shook his head doubtfully. "It won't do," he said. "There's somethin' you're keepin' back, Jeremiah. You've always been fair and square with me, old man; what's started ye off?"

Jeremiah heaved a deep sigh. "You always was as curious as a woman," he said.

"I reckon it's a good failin' to resemble 'em as much as we can," Sam remarked, placidly; "they generally get there."

Jeremiah had opened a small black trunk which stood in one corner of the room, and taken out a white pasteboard box. He removed the cover and displayed a quantity of very old and yellow popcorn, which was running out of a torn, crumpled paper bag.

"It's on account of this bag o' pop-corn I'm goin' home," he said; "all on account of this."

"What!" gasped Sam, confirmed in his suspicions that Jeremiah had taken leave of his senses. "Goin' East on account of a bag of pop-corn! Man, are you crazy?"

"I shouldn't wonder if I was," Jeremiah said, calmly; "but I'm goin', Sam, nevertheless. Don't look at me like that. I'll tell you about that popcorn. It wasn't just the bag of pop-corn, 't was somethin' more. 'T was a note, Sam, a note that went with it, writ to me thirty years ago." From his breast pocket he carefully drew a rumpled piece of paper, which he regarded mournfully, while Sam watched him in amazement. Then he held it out to Sam with a trembling hand. "I guess I may as well let you read it, since it was thirty years ago," he said. "You'll find the writin' pretty much faded," he added, drawing the back of his hand across his eyes.

Sam took the letter, and, searching in his pocket, succeeded in securing a pair of spectacles, which he slowly adjusted, and then fixed his most profound attention upon the scrap of paper.

"I don't mind your readin' it out, now you're at it," Jeremiah timidly suggested; and with a good deal of difficulty his friend deciphered the following:

DEAREST JEREMIAH: Knowing your liking for pop-corn, I put this note at the bottom of the bag, feeling sure that you'll not be long in reaching it; so you cannot be very far on your journey before you know that what I said last night was all a mistake. I didn't suppose you really meant it when you said you were going away. If I had I should have begged you not to go, for you must know that I do care for you, dear Jeremiah, more than for all the world besides. I know that you will forgive me and come back some time; and when you do, you will find me waiting, as ever, and forever yours,

AMANDA WELBY.

Sam took off his spectacles, and looked at Jeremiah. "Well, that's very pretty. But what's a note writ thirty years ago to do with your goin' off?"

"It seems to me you're mighty stupid," said Jeremiah, fretfully; "can't you understand, I never got it in all these long, long years?" and he sat down and buried his head in his hands.

"Well, I declare!" murmured Sam.

Jeremiah paced up and down the room with his hands in his pockets.

"Amanda Welby was the finest girl in all the county," he went on, excitedly; "all the boys were after her, to take her to the fair, or to the circus, or to see her home from meetin'. But somehow she always seemed to rather take a particular shine to me, until I came to feel about sure that Amanda thought a good sight of my keepin' company with her; in fact, she'd as much as told me so once or twice. All at once I had a chance to go West and make my fortune, as they all said, and I thought I'd go for a while, as there was n't much of an openin' in Greenboro. When I came to spring it upon Amanda, I thought she did n't care, for she kind o' laughed and asked me 'why I s'posed she'd care so much about my goin' East or West.' I might have known she did n't mean it, after the kindness she'd showed me along of mother's funeral; but I was angry, and went home and packed up my things that night. In the mornin', just as I was startin' out, I saw her little cousin runnin' over with a bundle in his hand. 'Cousin Amanda said to be sure to give you this,' he called out. I snatched it from him and untied the string and looked inside. It was pop-corn! Amanda had sent me a bag of pop-corn! That was pretty tough. Addin' insult to injury, that's what it seemed to me. When I saw

him comin' over, I rather thought to myself that
she'd been a reconsiderin'; and when I laid eyes
on that pop-corn, I tell you I was mad.   I grabbed
the bag to throw it down in the road right there;
but on second thoughts I opened my valise and
tucked it in, to remind me of the heartlessness and
perfidy of women.   From that day to this I have
never tasted one grain of pop-corn, but I kept that
bag shut up in a box where it was a warnin' against
the whole lot.   If ever I saw a face that I liked
the looks of, I'd just go home and take off the
cover of that box, though 't warn't very often that
I did it, for I never saw any one t' attracted me as
Amanda did.   Well, I'd kind of begun to think I'd
stay here always, and I hadn't so much as seen
that old white box for years, when I come across it
a few days ago.   I was sortin' out some old things,
and the box fell out, and when I opened it the bag
was broken open, and the note was stickin' out of
it like the finger of fate.   Oh, Sam, to think of my
waitin' thirty years to read it!"

Sam rose and laid his hand on his friend's
shoulder.   "Don't excite yourself so, Jeremiah," he
said, "but think it over, calmly, and I reckon you'll
decide to stay here with your friends.   Don't go
back East just for sorrow and disapp'intment.
You can't calculate that any woman's been waitin'
around thirty years for you.   Most likely she took
up with the next one that come along."

"I don't know 's I'd blame her if she did," protested Jeremiah.

"And she may be dead and gone long afore this," Sam concluded solemnly.

Jeremiah bowed his head submissively.

His friend was silent for a few moments, and then ventured, "Don't you think you'd better make up your mind to stay with us?"

Jeremiah rose majestically. "Stay with you!" he exclaimed, almost scornfully; then noting his friend's grieved expression, he continued more gently: "I'm sorry to leave all of you folks here, but I wouldn't stay longer 'n it takes to get my things off, if you gave me every gold mine in this State, and the rest of the country thrown in!"

Those inhabitants of Greenboro, who had lived there for the past thirty years, and had witnessed the gradual changes going on around them during that time, could not easily have understood the emotions which struggled in the breast of Jeremiah Tufts as he slowly wended his way up the main street of the village and looked about him. The picture of the place as he left it had always remained clearly imprinted on his mind; and although in coming back he had prepared himself for a goodly number of improvements and changes, he had expected nothing like the transformation which greeted his eyes.

He turned his steps toward the old tavern, but on

reaching the spot he was confronted by a large modern hotel which was pervaded by an air of bustle and activity, and presented itself in all the doubtful glory of electric bells and bell-boys with brass buttons. The quiet composure of the old tavern, with its portly proprietor smoking his long pipe with his feet upon the piazza rail, was a thing of the past. Jeremiah surrendered his valise to a porter, and wrote his name submissively in an imposing register which one of the brisk clerks pushed towards him. After a late dinner served in a countless number of little dishes, he started out to make the acquaintance of this new Greenboro. The boyish enthusiasm which he had felt as he stepped lightly off the train was rapidly leaving him, and he walked slowly down the street, feeling that he was like the Greenboro of thirty years ago, a thing of the past. He saw a postman with a shiny bag going about distributing letters, and watched the bright electric cars which ran to the next town, rushing by him, until he began to question whether this was really Greenboro after all. Everywhere the old stores had disappeared and large blocks had arisen in their stead.

He caught a glimpse of the old burying-ground on the hill, however, which reassured him, and he turned his steps towards it. On the way he passed a new and thriving grocery store which bore on its sign a familiar name. He went in and asked if he could see Deacon Holden. The deacon had always been a good-natured man in whom Jeremiah had found a firm friend on many occasions when he and the other village youths had indulged in juvenile pranks. The clerk looked at him in astonishment and remarked coldly that " the old deacon had been dead these fifteen years." Jeremiah quite resented his calling the deacon old, for he thought of him as he had seen him last, in the prime of life, with his genial smile, measuring out sugar for his customers, and putting in a little extra after the scales tipped, instead of scooping some out as the clerk before him was doing.

Jeremiah walked sadly over to a counter where he saw a pile of pop-corn in bags, and, obeying the dictates of a contrite spirit, he bought a bag and strolled down the street eating some as he went. The flavor of it seemed to bring back, as if it were only yesterday, a night when he drove Amanda home from the county fair, by moonlight. He remembered what an ideal flavor the pop-corn had that he ate during that drive. This did not taste at all like it, and he thrust the bag into his pocket and strode towards the cemetery. He could not make up his mind to turn his steps towards the little white cottage which used to stand half a mile beyond, in the cross-road. He felt sure that he would find it gone or deserted, and learn that its former occupants were dead or scattered.

He entered the old burying-ground, appalled at the number of white marble slabs which had arisen to testify to the changes that thirty years had wrought in Greenboro. He walked to the upper end of the ground, where under, an old elm, he found one familiar spot. Here two simple slate tablets marked the resting-place of his mother and father. The lichens which covered the stones wholly obscured the lettering, but to Jeremiah all the letters presented themselves as clearly as when he first watched them cut upon the stones. He sat down on a little iron stool that he had placed there almost thirty-five years before, and looked affectionately at the old stones. Here, at all events, he felt at home.

Some one had kept the lot in perfect order. It was not overgrown with weeds like many others up in that old corner where the white marble was almost an unknown quantity, and Jeremiah wondered who could have planted myrtle on the two graves. Were there then some old friends who still felt an interest in his mother and father? He walked a short distance to the Welby lot, and then paused in fear, not daring to read the names on the additional stones there. But at last he nerved himself and stepped near enough to read the inscriptions. He read the names of Amanda's father and mother on two rather pretentious tablets, and then turned tremblingly towards a third and smaller stone.  It bore the name of Jerusha: she was Amanda's younger sister.  A wave of thankfulness swept over him; but it was only a momentary relief, for, as he threaded his way along an adjoining path, his eye fell upon another stone.  He stopped, and stood fixedly confronting it, while a cold chill crept over him as he read again and again the words : " Amanda, beloved wife of Ezra Parks, in the 27th year of her age."

Jeremiah dropped on his knees by the stone and buried his head in his hands.  So she had married Ezra Parks,— great awkward Ezra Parks.  Surely she never could have cared for him, for time and time again Jeremiah had heard her say she could n't bear the sight of him.  What would he not give to know whether those few short years had been happy ones.  He who had been her husband could never tell him ; for a few feet distant another stone marked the spot where Ezra himself had been laid nineteen years later.

Jeremiah pressed his lips against Amanda's name, cut in the cold slate.  " After thirty years I have come back, dear," he murmured.  " Oh, if I had only known it sooner !  It was cruel, too cruel ! Yes, I forgive you for marryin' him !  I know you waited — waited — for one word from me, which never came."  He turned away, bitterly, murmuring, " I will go back to the West.  Sam was right; there 's only sorrow and disappointment here ! "

He returned to his little iron seat, and sat there watching the sun go down. The glory of the sunset seemed to mock his loneliness; but the two mounds of myrtle brought him a sort of consolation, such as the actual presence of his mother and father might have brought him. At last he rose and started down the hill. As he passed Amanda's grave he thought how bare and deserted it looked; and he determined to bring some flowers to leave there before he went away.

He mechanically turned his steps towards the little white cottage. Perhaps it might be still standing, after all, and he might get some flowers from the well-remembered garden to put on Amanda's grave; she used to be so fond of the flowers in that garden; he turned a bend in the road, and suddenly came in sight of the small, white cottage. It looked the same, in every particular. Here, alone, nothing had changed, save the trees, which had grown so much taller and denser. Neat and trim seemed everything, with the same clusters of roses shading the porch; and as he neared the spot he could see that smoke curled up from the wide brick chimney; but no sound could be heard about the house except the chirp of the crickets. He remembered how, in the old times, of a summer evening, Mrs. Welby's pleasant face could be always seen on the little porch, as she sat with her knitting, while the three girls sat on the steps and chatted and laughed with

the friends who dropped in.    The flowers were
much as of old in the garden.    As Jeremiah approached the fence and looked over, a delicate odor
of mignonette was wafted towards him, which
seemed to efface those thirty years and make him
a boy again.

A slender figure was moving gently about, with a
watering-pot, at the end of the garden, and he stood
and watched her until his eyes grew misty; for
something in the way she moved reminded him of
Amanda.    He would at least go in and ask her if
he might have some flowers.    He opened the gate
and walked up the path, in the dusk, so quietly that
she did not hear him until he stood almost beside
her; then, as she suddenly turned to fill the watering-pot from a pail near by, she saw him standing
there, and, in her astonishment, she dropped the
watering-pot.    Jeremiah gallantly stooped and re-
stored it to her, while something, he knew not
what, brought his heart up into his mouth.

"I ask your pardon for comin' upon you so unexpected," he began, hat in hand; then he paused.

"It was a bit sudden," she said, a little nervously,
and beginning to tremble, she could not tell why.

Surely, he thought, her voice is very like
Amanda's.

"I wanted to get a few flowers to put on a grave
in the buryin'-ground," he went on, "and I thought,
if you did not consider it too great a liberty, I'd ask

"'FOR HEAVEN'S SAKE, BE YOU AMANDA?'"

you to give me just a—" He stopped and gasped, "For heaven's sake, be you Amanda?"

Some familiar tone in his voice made her start, and she came a step nearer.

"Yes, I am," she replied, hesitatingly, "though there's few to call me Amanda now. And you?" she questioned, doubtfully.

Jeremiah seized both her hands. "Amanda," he cried, "look at me hard. Don't you know me? Ain't there a speck of the old look left?"

He held her hands with a grip like iron, while she trembled from head to foot. At last her lips moved, and she murmured: "It can't be,—it can't be; he's dead long ago,—Jeremiah's dead."

"I'm not dead, Amanda," Jeremiah cried, throwing his arms about her, "I've come back to you. I'm alive,—I'm as live as they make 'um,—I'm a sight liver 'n I ever was before. And I love you better than ever, Amanda; and that's why I've come back."

Amanda's fixed and stony gaze had changed, as he spoke, to ecstasy and tears, and she dropped her head on his shoulder, sobbing, "The Lord forgive my unbelief, Jeremiah. I had given ye up."

They sat down on the same old steps where they used to sit thirty years before, and he told her all about it, how all those years he never had read the note.

"Amanda," he sighed at last, "when life is so

short, I can't understand why such things are allowed to happen."

She wiped her eyes, which seemed brighter than ever, though her locks were streaked with silver. "Jeremiah," she said, "'t was the will of the Lord. Let us only remember His mercy, which brought us together."

Then he told her how he had suffered up in the old burying-ground on the hill. "I was sure you was dead," he said, "for I read Amanda Parks on a stone, and I thought you had married him; and I could n't much blame you if you had."

"Jeremiah," she said, reproachfully, "how could you possibly think such a thing of me? Had n't I said if you ever came back you would find me waitin'? In all the years that I looked for your comin', I never once thought that of you, but always said, if he does n't come back, he is dead; and you believed, because his wife's name was Amanda, that I had gone and married that Ezra Parks!"

Jeremiah bowed his head. "Amanda," he said, "you must remember, I'm only a poor weak man, not up to the high ideals of the wimmen. As my old friend, Sam Wilkins, says, I guess the best we can do is to try to resemble 'em as much as we're able."

He drew from his pocket the bag of pop-corn which he had bought in the village, and they shared it, half laughing, half weeping, while in the dusk, which hid the silvery threads in the two heads so near each other, no one would have dreamed that thirty long years had elapsed since they ate their last pop-corn together.

# THE ROMANCE OF A SPOON

# THE ROMANCE OF A
# SPOON

IT was rumored that Miss Helen Maryland was
to give a small and select dance very shortly —
invitations to which, it was well understood, were
most desirable. All social gatherings at the Marylands' were well attended, and young and old
esteemed it a privilege to spend an evening beneath
their hospitable roof-tree.

Mrs. Maryland was mistress of the art of entertaining, and her daughter Helen had inherited her
mother's easy cordiality and pleasing manners,
while her own sincerity and frank good - nature
would doubtless have made her the general favorite that she was had her father's dollars been but
few and her mother's delightful parties not at all;
though who knows? popularity is such a very dependent sort of thing.

Information about the forthcoming dance, which
would have very much surprised Miss Maryland
herself, was rapidly circulated, — by nobody in particular and everybody in general, — while she sat
intent upon the game of progressive euchre which

was going on among the party of young people
assembled in Mrs. Welsh's pretty drawing - room.
Helen Maryland was, in fact, not aware that any
one but her most intimate friend, Linda Walford,
knew that she cherished the thought of shortly
entertaining some of her friends, and her own ideas
on the subject were decidedly indefinite.    She
might have ascertained, however, from bits of conversation floating about the room, that the dance
was to be on such an evening, and at such a time;
that the music was to be thus, and the supper so;
and many other interesting items equally edifying,
and of which she was blissfully ignorant.

At the head table, George Marlowe and his
friend Forrester Wells had arisen from their chairs,
about to part company.    George was going down
to the foot table.

"Good-by, old fellow," he was just remarking.
"I'll see you later in the evening."

"I say, who is the coming lady, George?" inquired his friend.

"Why, the very girl I told you was going to give
a swell dance."

"Good!    Introduce me — quick! before you go.
My partner has gone to speak to Mrs. Welsh, and
she always takes it for granted that every one
knows every one else; and it is not the slightest
use for me to hum and haw, and wink and shuffle
the cards."

At this juncture, Miss Maryland appeared on the scene, and Marlowe hastily presented his friend and departed.

Wells at once set about making himself as agreeable as possible, and he could be very agreeable when he chose. This evening kind fortune smiled upon him in the form of an immediate announcement of supper, for which he at once secured Miss Maryland as his partner.

"I have heard Mr. Marlow speak of you so often that I feel as if we were almost old friends," he began, when they were snugly ensconced upon the stairs; "and," he added, "he promised to ask if he might bring me to call some time; but I am afraid he is not to be depended upon. I suspect he wants to monopolize you himself."

This was stretching the truth just a trifle, as Forrester had stoutly refused to make any calls whatsoever with his friend upon several occasions.

"I may get the better of him now," he added, gaily, "if you will let me come on my own hook. I sha'n't depend upon him any more after this."

Helen found him very entertaining, and it was rather flattering to feel that she had really made such an impression upon George Marlowe's handsome friend. And so it happened that Forrester Wells received, during the following week, a dainty invitation to the Maryland mansion for Wednesday, the 27th.

"So much for making myself very agreeable," he remarked, with great satisfaction, to Marlowe.

"So much for having a large amount of cheek and unlimited assurance," promptly responded his friend.

Miss Maryland's cotillon — for such it resolved itself into — proved a great success. Music, floor, supper, and society, all of the best, and that kind of "best which is not the cheapest."

Forrester Wells meditated upon the golden opportunities which were often lost through short-sightedness, as he straightened his tie in the dressing-room, just before supper. He was always very particular about his neckties. Then he went downstairs, and asked Miss Fanny Marlowe if he might have the pleasure of taking her out to supper. She was George's sister, and he offered this sacrifice upon the altar of his affection for George, as she was not generally considered very attractive.

There was some compensation offered, however, by the fact that he knew her so well, and she never cared for anything but a little ice-cream (so different from George), and then she was quite willing to sit and talk to the next girl for an indefinite time, while he enjoyed himself elsewhere. It was, after all, really much better than taking one of the belles out to supper, he reflected, for they were apt to be very exacting, although there was always that certainty of plenty of other men coming up to talk and pass things when one wanted to go and get a few mouthfuls himself.

He now deliberately helped Miss Marlowe to ice-cream, a process rendered quite simple by the fact that all the others were intent upon getting salad and oysters. Then he tried to remember which she preferred, a spoon or a fork. He thought she preferred a spoon, but Miss Maryland was sitting beside her, and she would probably consider it more elegant to bring a fork, so he took both. Presenting the plate of ice-cream with one hand, while he held the other behind him, he inquired :

" Which will you have, a spoon or a fork ? "

To which she replied, " A fork, if you please."

This he produced, with a flourish. " See how I read your thoughts ! " he exclaimed, deftly slipping the spoon into his coat-tail pocket, until he should have a chance to return it to the table.

Then he allowed his thoughts to turn in the direction of his own supper, which he modestly began with a few raw oysters, and the spoon was quite forgotten. Wholly unconscious of its existence, he was among the last to bid his hostess good-night ; and, thanking her for a most delightful evening, which had some time since ceased to be evening at all, he took his departure.

He set out briskly on his walk of a mile and a half home, there being no car at this time of night. He had gone fully half a mile, when a thought of the unlucky spoon presented itself, and he stopped as though he had received an electric shock. Here was a pretty how-d'ye-do! Going off with a silver spoon in his pocket. What a story for the fellows to get hold of! No danger of that, however; and he obeyed his first impulse to take it back at once, by beginning to retrace his steps immediately. Probably some of the guests were still there. Almost always there were some intimate friends who stayed to talk things over.

Here he began to run. What a fool he was to be so forgetful! Why had n't he brought Miss Marlowe her ice-cream with a spoon in the first place, or a fork, instead of giving her a choice? So much for being over-polite. What should he say when he got back to the house? Why, that he had forgotten something, of course; left something in the dressing-room. Then only to rush up-stairs, and leave the spoon anywhere — on the table or the bureau — where it would be easily found. No one would dream who had left it there. It was really very humiliating for a fellow like him, who prided himself upon always doing the correct thing, to carry off a silver spoon in his pocket, and yet he realized how inexpressibly funny it would have seemed if Marlowe had done it. What a very uninteresting girl Fanny Marlowe was! He could not understand how George could have such a stupid sister.

Yes, this was the house ; but how changed ! All the brilliant illuminations turned to darkness. Apparently every gas-jet in the house extinguished, save a faint glimmer up-stairs. How could a half-hour or so have made such a difference ? He had not dreamed that they would turn the lights out so soon. It was no use, now, to ring the bell, and he slowly turned upon his heel, and started once more toward home, though in a frame of mind not the most amiable.

Mrs. Maryland was a thoroughly systematic house-keeper, and after any entertainment which she gave always took account of stock, so to speak. Being blessed with a long-trusted waitress, who each night locked up the silver and brought her the key of the safe, she gave herself no uneasiness in this direction. Jane, however, having been occupied until the last moment the previous evening, putting on wraps and overshoes for the young ladies, had en-trusted this important mission to the parlor-maid, who had massed the silver together, and locked it up, regardless of any sorting out whatever. So it happened that Mr. Maryland balanced his coffee-spoon in hand the next morning, and remarked that he had one of great-grandmother Meade's best teaspoons. And so it came about that Mrs. Mary-land, herself, sorted them out after breakfast, saying that she would put them in a separate drawer in the safe.

And then she suddenly discovered that one of them was missing. There were only eleven. Where was the twelfth? Those spoons were the apple of Mrs. Maryland's eye, with their antique handles and old-fashioned monogram. That spoon must be found. There was certainly great carelessness among the servants. Thereupon followed a tempestuous morning below stairs, with threats from the cook to leave at once, in spite of an impending dinner-party that evening. It was very strange, but the spoon could not be found, and after a day or two the subject dropped, only to be revived by an occasional feeble joke, on Mr. Maryland's part, about Helen's friends admiring the pattern of the teaspoons.

When Forrester reached his room, he took out the spoon and scrutinized it. Yes, it was a very handsome one, probably some of the old family silver, and it would be missed at once. How would it do to send it right back by mail? That might be risky; things were so often lost in the mail. No; he would go around with it after his first lecture in the morning. He would make them an early call, and the whole thing would pass off as a good joke. Rather too good a joke, probably, as Miss Maryland would enjoy telling the story to numerous friends, and when the fellows got hold of it they would never let the thing rest; he wouldn't, himself, if Marlowe had done it.

He laid the spoon carefully upon a swinging shelf above his mantel, and then proceeded to retire, determined to solve the problem of how to return it most creditably in the morning.

When morning came, a loud knock rudely startled him from his slumbers, and before he could open his eyes a telegram was thrust into his face. It was a despatch from his mother, announcing that his sister Margaret was very ill, summoning him home at once. He had just time to dress and catch the next express westward, without even a thought of breakfast, only a hasty line scrawled to Marlowe, and left upon his table.

Marlowe roomed just across the hall from Wells, although it would have been hard to tell in which apartment he spent most of his time. On the following evening several congenial spirits were assembled in Marlowe's room to partake of a Welsh rarebit, the science of which he had mastered with an ease that did not characterize his treatment of the classics. His father, who could not seem to realize that a quarter of a century had elapsed since his own college days, regarded this fact as something almost disgraceful, which was more the pity, since Marlowe's understanding of Welsh rarebits had earned for him a wide-spread fame, which years wasted upon the classics never would have brought him.

Marlowe presided over the blazer with all the

dignity becoming so important a position. "Where's
my spoon, Warner?" he exclaimed, casting his eyes
over the necessary materials ranged about him on
the table.

"I haven't got it," returned that worthy individual, who was devoutly kneeling before a small
stove, in which gleamed a coal fire, with his entire
attention concentrated upon a slice of toast which
he held upon the end of a fork. "Do you think
I'm toasting bread with a spoon, George? It is
bad enough doing it with a fork minus a handle.
You can have this now, if you like," he added
amiably, sliding off the last slice of toast, which had
taken on a decidedly black tint during this conversation. "Here, Thompson," he concluded, tossing
it across the room to him, "just scrape off this
toast, will you, and make yourself useful while I find
the master of ceremonies a spoon?"

This Thompson proceeded to do with his pocket-
knife, resting the toast, meanwhile, on Marlowe's
German dictionary, while the owner thereof solilo-
quized:

"It's very queer where my spoon has gone to.
Perhaps you'll find it in Wells's room," he suggested, pausing with a slice of cheese in one hand,
and an egg in the other. "Skip in there, Thompson, and see, will you?"

As Thompson disappeared, somebody inquired,
"Where is Wells to-night?"

" He has gone home," responded Marlowe. " His sister is very sick, and they telegraphed for him this morning."

General expressions of sympathy were here interrupted by the return of Thompson, triumphantly waving a spoon in the air.

" Hello ! that's not my spoon ; mine is a bigger one," exclaimed Marlowe, taking it. " I never saw this before. Wells is going in for solid silver, and that's really a mighty pretty handle." With this he proceeded to the important business of making his Welsh rarebit a success.

A week later Marlowe was dining at the Marylands', being among the chosen few invited to meet a cousin who had come on from the West. The cotillon was several times referred to, and the cousin, next to whom he had the honor of being seated, turned to him, saying :

" I want you to tell me all about it, Mr. Marlowe. I am so disappointed that I did not come on in time for it." Marlowe proceeded to set it forth in glowing colors, ending off with a reference to " the most delicious supper."

" Yes," broke in Mr. Maryland, " and some of Helen's friends were so hungry that they began upon the spoons."

" Papa !" broke in Helen, reproachfully.

" Did n't they eat up one of grandmother Meade's teaspoons ? " he responded, laughing.

"What do you mean?" queried the cousin, who could never appreciate Mr. Maryland's jokes.

"Simply this," interposed Mrs. Maryland, with a sweet smile, which spoke to Mr. Maryland of disapproval, "one of the spoons disappeared that night — probably thrown away in the clearing up. It was like this, you know," she added, taking up one from beside her dessert-plate, "and, of course, we were sorry to have the set broken into; but we do not usually entertain our friends with details of this sort," she concluded, with a reproving glance at her husband. Then, with a view to changing the subject, she turned to Marlowe, saying: "We were very much pleased with your friend Mr. Wells the other night. He is a very interesting fellow, and I hope we shall see more of him."

What could have so disconcerted the usually self-possessed Marlowe? He seemed very much embarrassed about something, and sat with his eyes riveted upon his dessert-spoon, murmuring something about Wells's having gone home on account of sickness — a very simple statement, the utterance of which should not have given him any trouble. Miss Maryland glanced up at him in surprise. Was he jealous of his friend, or had he been quarrelling with him?

When he reached home that night, Marlowe hastily looked about him for something, which, not meeting his anxious gaze at once, he lighted all the

gas-burners and looked again for, but without success. Then he crossed the hall, and lighted all the
burners in the opposite room, and continued his
search, but in vain. He was very cross, and turned
things upside down, in a way which would have made
the orderly Wells's hair stand upon end could he
have looked in upon the scene, and had his hair not
already been in an upright position. Next, leaving
both doors open, he strode down the hall, and
thumped upon a door at the farther end.

"What's the matter?" responded a sleepy voice
from within.

"I want to see you. Open the door, will you,
Thompson?"

"Is that you, Marlowe? What do you want at
this time of night?"

"I want to see you, old man. Open the door,
sleepyhead."

With an audible groan, the door was unlocked,
and Thompson bounced into bed again. Marlowe
walked in and lighted the gas.

"Oh, turn that down, I say; you're blinding me!"
exclaimed the victim, burying his head in the
pillow. "Can't you talk to me without such an
illumination?"

"Thompson," began his persecutor, seating himself decidedly on the foot of the bed, "what did we
do with that confounded spoon that last night I
made the Welsh rarebit?"

"What!" exclaimed the victim, actually becoming wide - awake with astonishment. "Is that what you waked me up for, to find you an old spoon? Clear out with your old Welsh rarebits." And Thompson prepared to launch his pillow at his tormentor's head.

"Oh, I say, be reasonable, old fellow!" his friend remarked, soberly. "I want to talk to you. I tell you it's not late. You must have turned in right after dinner."

"Nonsense!" said Thompson, reaching over to his vest for his watch. "It's half-past twelve, and I've an examination early. But fire away and have it over with. The spoon was by way of introduction, I suppose. Speaking of spoons, is she dark or light, tall or short? I'm listening."

"Oh, hush up, Thompson! It's nothing of the sort. Do you think I've waked you up to talk nonsense of that kind?"

"Well, you have before. Only week before last you kept me awake for hours telling me that her eyes were perfectly wonderful and her hair was — "

"Will you keep quiet and let me talk, if you are so sleepy?"

"Yes, I will. But you need not call me sleepy now. You've spoiled my best nap and I shall probably stay awake the rest of the night."

Having reduced Thompson to a submissive mood, Marlowe began his recital. When he had finished, silence reigned for a few moments. Then Thompson ventured:

"Are you certain that spoon had the same pattern on it?"

"I'm almost positive, but I want to make sure, and I can't find the spoon. I thought that perhaps you had borrowed it."

"No, indeed. I have n't seen it since that night."

"And that was the very night after the Marylands' party," mused Marlowe. "Still I can't imagine any fellow putting up a joke of that sort on people he scarcely knew. It 's not a bit like Wells; but it is the strangest thing I ever heard of, and something that no gentleman could do. Yet if he did, think how I feel to have been the one to introduce him and answer for him, and I would certainly have answered for him anywhere!

"When it came across me at dinner it almost choked me to think that I had been deceived all this time, and that Forrester was not the fellow that I took him for. It was such an unmistakable pattern, you know. I never saw anything like it. I don't believe I could forgive him for a joke of that sort."

"Perhaps some other fellow put it in his pocket for a joke on him," suggested Thompson.

Marlowe shook his head mournfully. "That 's not very likely. No; Forrester has always had a craze for collecting trophies of every kind, and this only shows that he has not the taste to put a limit to that sort of thing. And now," he concluded, despairingly, "where has the spoon gone? Good-night, Thompson," and, putting out the light, his friend banged the door and departed without further ceremony to his own room, where, before retiring, he spent some time longer in thoroughly turning things upside-down in a vain search for the missing spoon.

Thompson was calmly disposing of ham and eggs the next morning, when Warner, who occupied a seat beside him at table, came in.

"Why didn't you come up to my room last night?" he began. "We had a rarebit that knocked Marlowe's higher than any kite."

"I wanted a little sleep last night," replied Thompson, helping himself to a third egg.

"I stopped for Marlowe, too," continued Warner, "but he had gone out to dinner, so I borrowed his spoon, and — what are you choking about?"

"Over excitement at hearing you tell such interesting details, Warner. By the way, Marlowe waked me up at midnight looking for that spoon."

"Is that so?" Well, I never saw a fellow who could take as many Welsh rarebits as he can. Has he been down to breakfast yet? I brought this spoon down in my pocket to return to him," he con-

tinued, producing it. "So I hope he'll appear before I have to skip."

"I'll see that it is returned," Thompson volunteered, quite eagerly.

"All right; much obliged." And Warner, having
swallowed the remainder of his coffee, rushed away,
leaving his friend, who never hurried his breakfast,
to finish that repast in peace.

"Yes, I'll return it," mused Thompson. "But,"
he concluded, a bright thought suddenly striking
him, "not to Marlowe — no, not to Marlowe."

And so it came about that soon after breakfast
he might have been seen directing a small, neat
bundle, with which he entered the post-office a little
later, wearing the same mischievous smile which
usually illuminated his comely face.

Forrester Wells returned the next afternoon in
high spirits, having left his sister on the fair road
to recovery. His time at home had been so fully
occupied that no ghost of the silver spoon had
troubled him until it recurred to his mind as he
opened the door of his own room once more. He
put down his bag, and looked about. "George has
been arranging things here," he commented, mentally; then he reached up to the swinging shelf
for the spoon. It was gone. In vain he looked
everywhere about the room; it was not to be
found.

While he was still occupied in this way Marlowe

appeared, and he called out, gaily, " Hello, George ;
here I am again ! "

" So I see," remarked his friend, without his usual
enthusiasm.    " How is your sister ? "

" Oh, much better.   By the way, did you see a
silver spoon around here after I left ? "

Marlowe eyed him sternly before responding.
" Yes, I think I did see one here.   Where did it
come from ? "

Wells resisted his first inclination to explain the
full particulars, and replied, carelessly : " Oh, I
picked it up somewhere.   It is a very convenient
thing to have about, you know.   It was a pretty one
with a fancy handle."

" Not the kind that you pick up in the street,
eh ? " put in George, scornfully.

" I hope that no one has walked off with it," continued Wells, without noticing the other's tone.
" It was an old-fashioned one, and I could n't get
another like it, you know."

" Not where you got that one," broke out Marlowe, with such vehemence that his friend suddenly
turned and faced him in astonishment.

" What do you mean ? " he demanded.

" Just what I say," returned the other, excitedly.
" I never believed you capable of such a thing.   I
thought that you were a very different sort of fellow.
Oh, Forrester, how could you ?   Is it a joke to carry
off silver from a house where you are being enter-

tained for the first time? That would be disgraceful enough; but if, still worse, you are merely pursuing a craze for trophies to be satisfied at any cost, please remember that when I present you to my friends, I hold myself responsible for your ungentlemanly conduct."

During this outburst Forrester's face was an interesting study of rapidly changing expression. First of complete astonishment and surprise, followed by incredulity; and then grieved amazement, as his friend's suspicion dawned upon him, and ending in a flash of haughty anger at the close.

As Marlowe paused, he strode to the door and threw it open. "You have said enough to convince me of your friendship," he exclaimed. "Now be kind enough to go."

Beneath his clear, penetrating glance, Marlowe's suspicions melted away, leaving him most penitent for his hasty words, and only desirous to atone for the injustice they had expressed.

"Indeed, I shall not go until everything is explained. Forgive me, Forrester, for doubting you. I know that you are and always have been the soul of honor. When you hear my side of the story you will see that there is some excuse for me."

Forrester's anger gradually subsided under this earnest appeal. "First," he said, "you must hear my terrible confession of guilt." And he briefly

recounted his experience, and his vain attempt to
return the spoon that night. "And, of course, you
know that I was telegraphed for next morning," he
concluded.

George, who was by this time contrition itself,
then told his story. How he borrowed the spoon;
all about the dinner-party; when he had seen the
spoons just like it; and last and worst, how the
spoon could not be found. Forrester whistled
thoughtfully.

"I am responsible for it," Marlowe insisted. "I
borrowed it, and I shall go and explain to the
Marylands all about it, and see if I can't have
another one made like it."

"Nonsense!" replied his friend; "you shall do
nothing of the kind, and I believe we shall find the
spoon yet. Suppose we go into your room, and
have one more thorough search?"

With this the two friends went manfully to work.
Forrester carefully turned over, scrutinized, lifted up,
and shook everything; while George kicked things
over, emptied out drawers, and never paused in his
mad career until the room looked as if it had been
suddenly struck by a cyclone. Every now and then
one of them remarked, "Oh! here is that match-
safe you lost so long ago;" or, "I've just found
that pearl scarf-pin of mine."

George finished up by emptying the contents of
his bureau drawers upon the bed, where collars and

handkerchiefs, neckties, cigarettes and stockings, tennis-caps and scarf-pins all mingled in glorious confusion.

" What did you do that for?" remonstrated Forrester. " I had just looked carefully through all those drawers, and now you've mixed things up finely."

" Oh, that's all right!" exclaimed George, cheerfully. " I just like to make sure, you know. It is the strangest thing where that spoon went to," he added, inspecting the coal-hod. " I declare, I've looked in every place I can think of, and found everything else that I ever lost, and I'm afraid we shall have to give it up."

It was with a step less elastic than usual that Forrester Wells mounted the Marylands' steps late that afternoon, while George Marlowe, by his side, assumed an air of extreme gaiety, which, nevertheless, failed to disguise the fact that he was just a little nervous and uncomfortable; the whole affair seemed so ridiculous and unnecessary, and so strongly recalled his very juvenile days when his father made him ring the gentleman's door-bell, and tell him that he had broken his window, but would be most happy to pay for it.

Miss Maryland was at home and welcomed them most cordially. They talked on all imaginable subjects, from music to football, none of which seemed to lead toward the subject which both young men were so anxious to introduce, not too abruptly, but in an easy and off-hand way.

Wells was cudgelling his brains for just the right sort of introduction, though it seemed to Marlowe that he had forgotten all about the spoon, and was going to talk on forever about some canoeing trip that he took the previous summer. Marlowe himself grew so abstracted as to actually jump when Miss Maryland unexpectedly addressed a remark to him. Why under the sun does n't Wells begin about that spoon? he was mentally ejaculating, when his attention was arrested by a portion of Miss Maryland's conversation.

" It was really very singular, and quite like something you read of in stories," she was saying. " You may remember, Mr. Marlowe, that we told you about a missing teaspoon that disappeared the night of the cotillon ? "

" Why, yes," murmured Marlowe, faintly.

" Well," she continued, " do you know, it came back to us through the mail this very morning? It is the most mysterious thing I ever heard of, and we have racked our brains in vain for a solution of the problem. Now, Mr. Wells, I am anxious to hear your theory on the subject ? "

Wells, who had hitherto been unusually quiet, found his animation suddenly returning. " How very interesting!" he exclaimed; " and how much more delightful not to solve the mystery! Mysteries are apt to prove so very prosaic when some one steps in and explains them, spoiling the story and taking away the romance. Come, Marlowe, we must be going. If we stay any longer, Miss Maryland will never want to see us again."

When the door closed behind them, Wells restrained his wild desire to execute an Indian wardance on the sidewalk, while Marlowe could not find words to express his satisfaction and delight at the turn affairs had taken.

" I 'll wager that Thompson will tell me something about that spoon when I see him," he broke forth.

" Since I know that it 's returned, I don't care a rap how it got there," gaily responded Wells. " There was something really providential in our beating about the bush all that time before we introduced the weighty subject. George, old man, I tell you it pays to own up like a gentleman. Be good and you 'll be happy, even if your friends don't have a first-rate time in consequence."

" Forrester," exclaimed his friend, putting his hand impressively on his arm, " you not only possess most unlimited cheek, as I 've told you before, but you have more confounded luck than any fellow I ever saw."

# THE HISTORY OF A HAPPY THOUGHT

# THE HISTORY OF A HAPPY THOUGHT

AND the thought was this — I would ask all my young friends from the neighboring cottages to bring around their various musical instruments, and we would spend a jolly, informal evening on my wide, airy veranda. I knew that my young cousin Josephine had found her stay with me extremely quiet, and I determined to do a little something to make things a trifle more lively, and so I drove about our summer colony inviting all my young friends who possessed banjos, guitars, etc., to bring them over in the evening. When I reached home, happy in the consciousness of well doing, I was greeted by a telegram, announcing that my husband would bring down with him on the five o'clock boat, two of our stiffest and most ceremonious English friends, Mr. and Mrs. Beresford-Pierce.

I looked at Josephine in dismay. "What shall I do about those banjos? It is after five now, and I have n't time to send them word not to come, and yet I would n't for the world have the Beresford-Pierces think that I had specially invited such a

collection of extraordinary young musicians to entertain them.  They are both intensely and critically
musical, so that it would not do, still, I have just
time to see that the cook gives us a little something
to eat, and you must help me to arrange some flowers; we must explain to them just how it happened,
and no doubt the young folks will prefer to talk
most of the time."

After our guests had been duly escorted to their
room, however, I hastened to inquire what my husband thought of the prospective music.  He seemed
much pleased at the idea, and declared that it was
certainly a most "happy thought;" it's just the
sort of thing they will enjoy, he assured me; and
he hurried away without giving me a chance to explain that I had not invited all the banjos after I
received his message.  Charlie hasn't a bit of tact,
at all events, and when, at dessert, the conversation
drifted towards music, he announced, with a reassuring smile at me, that I was planning to have
some music after dinner.

Our guests seemed much pleased at the prospect,
and Mrs. Beresford-Pierce said, dreamily, "that they
had not heard any good music since they left
London."  I hurriedly explained that we were
merely expecting a few young friends with guitars
and banjos, and assured them that it would not be
classical music with which they would be apt to
favor us, but our English friends insisted that it

would be a "great treat." We were finishing our coffee when the Emmonses arrived with their banjos.

"Now, Fred, you and Tom can give us some tunes before the others come over," I suggested, as we adjourned to the piazza.

"I think we had better wait until the others get here," he replied; "but we will tune up while we are waiting. Give me your third string, Tom," he added.

"Let me get in tune first," responded Tom. "I put on some new strings this afternoon, and they are all off." It was quite evident from his efforts to bring them back that they were a long way off, but at last they seemed to give satisfaction, at which point Fred proceeded to repeat the process, varying it, however, by two loud snaps.

"Strings do not last long at the seashore," he announced, cheerfully selecting new ones with great deliberation. "You are tuned up too high, Tom; you must come down, or I shall break every string I own."

I called Mrs. Beresford-Pierce's attention to the lights in the harbor, and I was glad to note that Charlie was indicating the points of interest to her husband. Meanwhile, Tom proceeded to "come down" without evincing that rapidity which usually characterizes a descent from any elevated position. They declared a moment later that they were in perfect tune — a fact which I saw that our guests apparently doubted; nevertheless, I hastened to say, " Do play some of your quaint darkey melodies."

" We can give you ' Swanee River,' or a jig," Tom replied, and as I remarked that the jig would be nice, I perceived three figures advancing across the piazza, and I recognized Mrs. Brown and her two nephews.

" I am glad to see some more of my orchestra," I called out, gaily, though I had been devoutly hoping that something would prevent their coming.

" Are they really an organized orchestra?" Mrs. Beresford-Pierce questioned, gravely.

" Oh, no," I explained, " they have never played together until this evening," and then, after introducing the Browns, and finding chairs for them, I begged the musicians to begin.

The young Browns had brought a piccolo and a banjoine, which they at once began to tune vigorously, while we sat patiently by. The piccolo was determined not to harmonize with the banjos, and I could see that Mrs. Beresford-Pierce's finely-trained nerves were undergoing exquisite torture, while her husband sat regarding the musicians with a fixed and wondering gaze. Even Charlie was getting impatient. " Let us have that jig," he cried out. The Emmonses asked the Browns if they knew it, but they said they did n't, but could n't the others play " The Invincible Guards' March?" No, they had never learned that. After a long consultation, they agreed to try the " Spanish Fandango," which they actually started ; by the time they reached the second variation, one of the Browns broke a string, and during the pause which ensued, Rose Elwood appeared with her guitar, and accompanied by her brother.

" I had great difficulty in persuading Harry to bring his bones over," Rose announced. " Ah ! what fun it is to have so many instruments together," she concluded, joining the orchestra, while Mrs. Beresford-Pierce, whose knowledge of "bones" was confined to her acquaintance with physiology, looked curiously at Harry. Just then I overheard Rose saying, "Let me have your third string, Mr. Emmons, it always takes me so long to get this guitar in tune."

Charlie was walking up and down with his hands in his pockets. " Play something, play anything, my friends," he exclaimed. " This suspense is wearing us out, I assure you."

As the tuning still continued, I suggested that perhaps it would be wiser for the audience to go inside, since it was growing rather cold; "and you musicians can come in when you are ready to play," I added, noting with satisfaction that Charlie had taken Mr. Beresford-Pierce to the farther end of the piazza for a quiet smoke.

We had hardly settled ourselves near the blazing

wood-fire in the hall for a quiet chat before the door opened, and our musical friends appeared, announcing that " it was no use trying to tune up outside where it was so damp." I looked mournfully at the other ladies. Mrs. Brown was smiling serenely; she lived in the house with the piccolo and the banjoine. Not so Mrs. Beresford-Pierce; she was trying to smile, but without success, and I could see that she was suffering acutely.

" Let me have your second string," the banjoine was saying to the guitar. The piccolo was endeavoring to reach the new pitch, and the banjos were tumming experimentally, while Harry Elwood kept time with the bones. All the musicians were serenely happy and quite unconscious of the fact that the rest of us were not provided with instruments to tune.

" Are n't we to have some music?" I queried, in a tone which might have been defined as bitter-sweet; but at that very moment I heard Arthur Brown protesting, " I cannot tune my piccolo up to that last key, so you will all have to come down a little."

" What! are we still tuning?" questioned Charlie, in comic dismay, as he ushered in Mr. Beresford-Pierce. I nodded. Alas! I thought feebly to myself, if it were only "still" tuning; but it is such painfully loud tuning.

And the worst of it was that my guests were

under the impression that I had asked in all these strange, unmanageable instruments on purpose to entertain them. At that moment I could have wept freely. Then I rallied and pulled myself together. I crossed the room and touched the electric bell, at which signal Jane appeared, bearing a tray with cake and ices.

" Now, suppose we have a little intermission," I announced, and my impromptu orchestra relinquished their instruments, though a trifle regretfully; they were enjoying it so much. We finished our ices in peace, and, having taken things into my own hands, I determined not to relinquish my advantage, so I spoke up boldly, " We will not try the orchestra all together again this evening," I said, " but we will hear them in sections, and will begin with ' The Invincible Guards' March,' by the two Mr. Browns, followed by their choicest waltz." They accomplished these selections successfully, after which the Emmons boys, accompanied by the bones, played a jig which quite brought down the house, and even necessitated an encore. Then Rose sang two very charming ballads with her guitar, which sounded so sweetly that Mrs. Beresford-Pierce thawed completely, and told Rose that she really ought to have her voice cultivated, and she only wished that she could take lessons of her teacher in London. Rose forbore to mention the fact that she had been faithfully trying to cultivate her voice for two years, and

only begged that Mrs. Beresford-Pierce would sing
something. After some demurring, she finally gave
us " Robin Adair " in a clear, rich voice, while Rose
played an accompaniment timidly on her guitar.

From this moment our English friends seemed to
be really enjoying themselves, and we all entered
into the college songs with great enthusiasm. I
noted with surprise that all the instruments were
actually going at once and seemed to be in pretty
good tune. Mr. Beresford-Pierce was heard to
whistle "Annie Laurie" with variations, while
Charlie went so far as to execute an Irish jig. I
glanced at our English guests to see if they were
shocked, but was reassured when, a moment later,
Mr. Beresford-Pierce volunteered that he knew something about a Scotch hornpipe himself, which he
performed, after some urging, to the stirring strains
of the banjos and bones. This crowning event called
forth a burst of applause which bespoke a truly appreciative audience, and when several of the musicians declared that it was time to go, I was
astonished to learn how late it was. My musicale
had been a success after all, I meditated, as I laid
my weary head on my pillow, but I must explain in
the morning that such an entertainment was wholly
accidental. Possibly they may have enjoyed it, I
said to myself, but they shall not go away from here
thinking that when I knew they were coming I went
and invited in a lot of instruments which had never

played together before, by way of entertaining them.
My last words to Charlie were, "If I do not get
time to explain things at breakfast, you must
promise to tell them just how it happened on the
way up to town." Of course, he forgot all about it,
and never mentioned it during the whole long hour,
which it took them to sail up to the city, with twenty
minutes extra thrown in for fog, and he certainly
could n't have been showing them the points of interest, as it was so thick they could n't see six inches
ahead of them. I can't imagine what he could have
talked about all that time, but it could not have been
anything very interesting, for he could n't recall a
word that he had said, he assured me afterwards, so
I believe he read his paper all the time. And in
spite of all my efforts to do so, I could n't make
Charlie realize that my reputation as a typical
American hostess had been at stake.

A few weeks later, I read aloud the following extract from a letter I had just received from a friend
at Newport: "Last week I had the pleasure of
meeting some delightful English people, who spoke
most enthusiastically of you, dear; they are Mr.
and Mrs. Beresford - Pierce, and they are being
greatly lionized here, on all sides. They spoke,
however, of an evening at your home by the sea,
which they considered, without exception, the most
charming that they had spent. Knowing how tre-
mendously they had been run after, I could not

help wondering what special attraction you had provided, you clever creature. When later, I had a chance to inquire, I learned that at the shortest possible notice you had provided a kind of impromptu orchestra, with banjos, guitars, etc. They said it was so charmingly spontaneous and unconventional that they considered it a typical American evening, which they should always look back upon with special pleasure. I envy your originality, dear, for who else would have thought of inviting in a collection of musical instruments of that sort on the spur of the moment, to entertain such very stiff English people."

I laid the letter down with a sigh, for I felt I had received rather a doubtful compliment, but Charlie was much pleased. "Good!" he exclaimed; "now, perhaps, you are convinced that it was 'a Happy Thought,' after all!"

# A FURNISHED COTTAGE
## BY THE SEA

# A FURNISHED COTTAGE
# BY THE SEA

MRS. BEAUFORT had declared herself tired
of hotel life, and had insisted that a furnished cottage was the only ideal place in which to
spend the summer. Her husband had finally been
brought to realize the overwhelming advantages to
be derived from such a plan, and had accompanied
her hither and thither in search of just the right
place.

They were not exacting in their requirements, but
Mr. Beaufort did feel that he would enjoy a ride
daily on a boat, in preference to the dusty train;
then his wife was anxious to have surf bathing near
by, and a pretty water view from the piazza; while
the daughters said they would be satisfied anywhere,
provided they had pleasant society and good sailing.

Simple as these requirements were, however, they
were eventually dispensed with, and, after many
trials and tribulations, a cottage was rented, which
had to be reached after an hour's ride by rail from
the city. Mrs. Beaufort must content herself with

still-water bathing and no ocean view; the girls had no congenial friends near by, and the sailing was not considered safe; but they had secured a furnished cottage, and they made up their minds to be content.

Even here, however, there was a modifying clause; for the cottage furnishings proved to be far from sufficient. There was no china to speak of, and they would have to take their own mattresses and almost all their cooking utensils, and rugs, and easy chairs, and lamps; besides several small tables, a small ice-chest, wash-tubs, bath tubs, pillows, and endless other things, not to mention necessities like the piano, Henrietta's davenport and her sister's dwarf bookcase.

When the large load of household belongings rolled away from the door, Mr. Beaufort said, doubtfully, "We've taken a good many things, considering that the house was fully furnished, my dear."

"Oh, it's just as well to be comfortable, while we are about it," his wife responded, cheerfully, "even if we do have to move a few more things back and forth."

"And after all, you won't have any rest from housekeeping," he continued; but she laughed lightly, "My dear, it will be a very much simpler matter keeping house at the seashore; things almost run themselves in a summer cottage, you know."

A few days later she wished devoutly that things

*would* run themselves, as she wended her way up to the city to secure a new cook and waitress who would be willing to put up with the great "unconvaniences." These were many and seemed to multiply rapidly. The roof leaked, the stove would not work, the cistern was so low that a man must daily bring water in pails for household use. Many greater and less evils Mrs. Beaufort discovered were apt to go with furnished cottages.

Then the company! Cousins, and aunts, and distant relatives galore, must be asked down for nice little visits, not to mention those who took it upon themselves to drop down unexpectedly at the least opportune moments. "All the people that I ought to want, as well as those I do want, must come," she said desperately; while Mr. Beaufort came home depressed and weary after his railroad trip, and the girls sighed for sailing and complained that there was nothing to do.

Mrs. Beaufort herself found that there was altogether too much to do. What with explaining how cooking could best be done on an oil-stove, and making sure that the water supply each day was sufficient, and sending up to town for fresh fish, and writing out lists for the washerwoman, and stepping out to the gate to view what the provision man had to offer; with these, in addition to the entertaining of Mr. Beaufort's second cousins and her own aunts, she found herself counting the days which must need

elapse before she could turn her face again towards
" home, sweet home."

But the happy day arrived at last, and, as she
watched the men piling up the last things upon the
wagon, she acknowledged to Mr. Beaufort that there
was more detail connected with renting a summer
cottage than she had ever believed possible.

" And I shall have to get new servants the same
as usual," she went on, mournfully, " as the cook insisted upon leaving yesterday, and Mary has just
heard of the death of her brother, which obliges her
to go at once, so we shall have to open the house
ourselves after all."

It was a bleak and raw afternoon when the Beau-
forts ascended their own front steps, laden with
bags, shawls, and many curiously-shaped bundles
suggestive of forgotten saucepans and stray coffee-
pots.

" It is time for the load to be here," Mr. Beaufort
remarked, as he unlocked the front door and
stepped inside.

" The house is as cold as a barn," Mrs. Beaufort
exclaimed, following him; " could that man have
forgotten to light the furnace fire to dry the house
off ?"

" Evidently he has," her husband responded; " but
I will start a fire here and in the kitchen at once,
myself."

Mrs. Beaufort wandered through the chilly rooms

in the deepening twilight; "I supppose it is better to be here a little while before the things arrive," she said, "so that we can look about somewhat. I hardly realized we took so many things away with us. I declare the house is quite empty."

The minutes slipped away and the darkness deepened, and still the welcome rumble of the express wagon was not heard. Again and again they looked anxiously out of the windows, but in vain. "I am *so* hungry," Henrietta declared; "but I don't suppose we can go out for our supper until that old load comes."

Mrs. Beaufort stood at one of the front windows, drawing her cape about her and shivering; "how strange that the man should not have come to start the furnace," she murmured.

"Papa is trying to light the kitchen fire," her daughter Kate put in, "so you can go out there and get warm."

"I don't think he understands anything about it," Mrs. Beaufort responded, hurrying toward the kitchen. She opened the pantry door, and through a mist of flying ashes she could dimly make out her husband's form, clad in what seemed to be a silvery gray suit. "Why, what are you doing?" she exclaimed, putting her handkerchief to her mouth.

"I am merely letting down the ashes, my dear," he answered, coughing. "I should think you would have had this cleared out before we went away. Can't you keep out of here until I get the fire started ? "

" But that is not the way to let the ashes down. Can't you see the room is filled with them, flying all over everything."

" If you will be kind enough to leave the kitchen, Clara," he returned, dusting his coat with his silk handkerchief, " everything will be all right ; " and he threw open two of the windows, making a draught which blew the ashes in clouds toward the pantry door.

At this moment Henrietta's voice was heard calling " Mamma, here is the wagon-load of furniture." " And it 's pitch - dark out here," Kate's voice announced.

Mr. Beaufort dropped the poker and hurried to the front door, followed by his wife. " Light the gas in the hall," he called to the girls.

" It won't light," they promptly responded, making way for two expressmen who stumbled in, laden with chairs and tables.

" What, hasn't the gas been turned on ? " Mr. Beaufort questioned ; " I sent them special word not to fail to have it on. Well, you will have to fly around and get some lamps lighted."

" I suppose you know that all the lamps are in the packing-trunks," Mrs Beaufort said regretfully.

" Well then, candles ; can't you find some candles?" Mr. Beaufort called back; "there must be some candles."

"I'm afraid we took all the extra candles with us," Mrs. Beaufort answered, hurrying into the store-room, while the girls ran hither and thither tumbling over the numerous pieces of furniture which the men were rapidly piling up in the hall.

After a frantic search, during which Mrs. Beaufort opened the pantry door and then ran against it, giving herself a black eye, one of the girls discovered a box filled with little colored candles such as are used on Christmas trees and birthday cakes. These were hastily brought out, lighted and set about in every available spot, where they dripped and sputtered fitfully.

"Tell the men to bring the three big packing-cases into the dining-room," Mr. Beaufort exclaimed, as he almost fell over a barrel of crockery which had been planted in the middle of the hall.

"Yes, the lamps are in one of those packing-cases, I'm sure," Mrs. Beaufort answered, breaking away from Henrietta, who was tying up her eye with a handkerchief wet in cold water.

"Girls, where are the keys to the packing-cases?" their father was saying, excitedly; "you remember you took them from me before we started."

"I gave them to mamma," promptly responded Kate, "and I don't know what she did with them."

"Mamma, what did you do with the keys?" she

called after her mother, who had gone in search of kerosene oil.

"Up-stairs in my black bag," came back from the laundry, where Mrs. Beaufort was wandering about with one Christmas-tree candle, which constantly burned her fingers with hot wax.

"Henrietta, show the men where to take those big square trunks," she added, coming in triumphantly with an oil-can, which her husband immediately kicked over in trying to move one of the packing-trunks.

As Henrietta disappeared up-stairs to pilot the big square trunks, a crash resounded through the house. "What is that?" Mrs. Beaufort cried, dropping the cloth with which she was wiping up kerosene oil from the dining-room hearth.

"Oh, mamma," came a voice from the darkness overhead, "the man has knocked down grandmother Hamilton's portrait with the corner of one of those trunks, on the way up-stairs."

Mrs. Beaufort drew a deep sigh, but did not speak; being only a woman no appropriate words instantly rose to her lips.

"And the glass is all over the stairs," her daughter's voice went on, encouragingly. This fact was quite evident from the crunching sound made by the descending feet of the two expressmen, who ground the well-distributed fragments into the hardwood floor below.

" And the floor has been newly done over, you know," she said to Mr. Beaufort. He, however, had no time to waste upon speculations of this sort ; he was down on his knees before one of the packing-cases trying to fit a key into its Yale lock. He had been all through the bunch once, without success, and had begun again, this time more slowly.

" Quick! they are bringing in the piano and we must have some light in the parlor," Kate was heard to exclaim, as a heavy thump against the hall wainscoting bespoke the entrance of that musical instrument.

Mr. Beaufort had succeeded in unlocking two of the packing-trunks, and he and Henrietta were plunging wildly into them to find the much-needed lamps. "That's the trunk with the table-linen in it, Henrietta," her mother said, coming into the room, "there are no lamps in there." This was already evident, as her daughter had reached the bottom after piling out the table-cloths and napkins in all directions on the floor.

" Here is part of the study lamp," Mr. Beaufort exclaimed, joyfully, throwing out armfuls of everything pell-mell.

" Where are the lamp chimneys? " Mrs. Beaufort queried.

" Right on top of one of the barrels," Mr. Beaufort replied, as a fourth barrel was rolled into the room.

"But *which* barrel?" his daughter called after him as he stepped into the hall. "This one seems to be all teacups," she continued, rapidly unrolling a number and setting them on the table.

"Here's the ice-cream freezer," Mr. Beaufort said, cheerily, setting it down directly on top of the teacups, which flew like chaff before the wind. "What under the sun do you want to go pulling out that china for yet?" he cried; "I should think there were enough things around already."

By the uncertain light of a blue, a yellow, and a red candle the men groped patiently for the legs of the piano, which they had great difficulty in adjusting. Kate stood beside them holding a candle in each hand, and shedding alternate streams of blue and red wax over her dress, the prostrate piano, and the bowed heads of the two expressmen, who finally retired after no worse mishaps than falling over one ottoman and upsetting the afternoon tea-table.

As Kate picked up the tea-caddy and ran her fingers over the surface of the brass kettle to ascertain how deeply it was dented, she saw her father standing triumphantly in the doorway holding a lighted lamp in his hands, which was smoking in a most lively way. "We've found some oil and we're all right now," he said, pleasantly. "Now we can see where we are."

This privilege seemed, however, rather a doubtful one, as the added illumination revealed anything but a cheerful view of their environment.

As the door closed behind the departing express-men, Mrs. Beaufort suggested, wearily, " If we can find that oil-stove, perhaps I can make a cup of tea, for I am too tired to go out anywhere for my supper."

Mr. Beaufort preceded her with the lamp, and they threaded their way cautiously over piles of table linen, broken china and the rest of the *débris* which covered the dining-room floor out into the hall, where grandmother Hamilton's shattered portrait looked reproachfully out from among hammock poles, bath tubs, and bundles of pillows and piles of rugs.

They entered the parlor, where the piano stood decorated by wax of many colors, and passed through into the sitting-room, where the oil-stove greeted their gaze; there it stood, safe and sound, in the centre of the polished mahogany table.

Having insisted that the others must go and get a substantial repast, Mrs. Beaufort sat alone in the midst of chaos. Barrels stood half unpacked about her, and broken china was under her feet, while the light from the lamp, which streamed dimly through the smoky chimney, revealed a wash-tub filled with cooking utensils resting upon the top of Henrietta's writing-desk.

Mrs. Beaufort silently watched the water in the

little saucepan on the oil - stove, which was almost boiling, as she drew from her luncheon basket, near by, a few crackers, the remains of their hasty lunch at noon.

On the dining - room table, beside the oil - stove, stood the ice-cream freezer, a waffle iron and a coal-hod, but Mrs. Beaufort saw them not; she looked across at a ghastly reflection in a mirror opposite. The mirror reflected a haggard face with a bandage over one eye — the eye which had come in contact with the pantry door.

As she gazed at the mournful spectacle, she murmured to herself: "I know not what punishment I have deserved for past misdoings, nor yet what fate the future has in store for me, but I devoutly hope I may not be called upon to expiate my sins by renting another furnished 'cottage by the sea.'"

# A HALLOWE'EN PARTY

VIEW OF BECK HALL, CAMBRIDGE.

# A HALLOWE'EN PARTY

THE writer smiled complacently as he penned the following lines: "Mr. J. Turner Dodge regrets that a previous engagement will prevent him from accepting Mrs. Horton's very kind invitation for Hallowe'en." Then he cheerfully directed an envelope, and after extracting a stamp from his letter-case, he caught up his hat and went forth to mail his note at once.

As the lid of the letter-box clicked after the descending "regret," J. Turner Dodge gave an audible sigh of relief and briskly retraced his steps to his rooms in Beck Hall. His return was hailed by his special crony, Charles Manhattan, who had come in to consult him about some vital question regarding athletics.

"What are you so pleased about?" his friend inquired, as he entered; "you look as if you had just received an extra check from the old man."

"I've been doing up my society correspondence," laughed the other; "by the way, are you going to do anything special next Monday night?"

Manhattan took out a small engagement-book and scanned it. "No, nothing for Monday night," he replied.

"Well, then, you have a pressing engagement to go to the theatre with me; we'll go anywhere you say. Now set it down and underline it three times, and put 'supper afterwards' in a big parenthesis."

After Manhattan had gone, his friend sat for some time gazing thoughtfully at the frost-nipped plants in the box outside of his window. A casual observer would have said that he was critically inspecting the condition of the drooping geraniums, but, in reality, at that moment he was totally unconscious of the existence of the vegetable creation.

J. Turner Dodge was inwardly reviewing his first Hallowe'en party; it was just a year ago that he had received an invitation from some suburban friends to spend that witching evening at their pleasant country house.

He knew the people only slightly, and the invitation seemed rather a formal one, but "Hallowe'en" sounded decidedly attractive. It savored of old-fashioned games and dances (of which his knowledge was very limited), and of thrilling ghost stories whispered to a spellbound circle about a blazing wood-fire. Therefore Dodge accepted the invitation immediately, undismayed by the fact that he must take a trip out of town, and he found himself looking forward to the prospective party with no little pleasure.

"They never have anything of the sort in New York," he remarked to his friend Thornton, who roomed near him; "nothing but the same old tiresome things over and over again."

That young gentleman grunted unsympathetically. "It may be the same old thing with a different label, my boy; at the last Hallowe'en party I went to, we played progressive euchre all the evening. There is the booby prize," he concluded, pointing to a many-colored drum suspended from his gas-fixture, and bearing the appropriate motto, "Something that you *can* beat."

This was a bit disheartening to Dodge, but he consoled himself with the thought that he always had pretty good luck at progressive euchre, after all.

He was in a particularly happy frame of mind on the eventful evening. The football team had been doing fine work all the afternoon, and he had been able to cut a large number of recitations successfully; then, his new dress suit had just come out from the tailor's and it fitted him perfectly. It had arrived exactly in the nick of time, he meditated, as his old one was really too shabby to be seen in. If Dodge had been a girl he would have gazed at himself in the mirror long and with undisguised admiration; being only a man, however, he merely glanced carelessly at his glossy-coated reflection a couple of times with tolerable complacency.

The first damper upon his high spirits he sustained when he reached the railway station, for as he strolled leisurely in to take the eight o'clock train, he was greeted by the announcement that the train had gone. "Eight o'clock train goes at seven minutes of, now," the man at the gate informed him with evident satisfaction; "just changed last Wednesday; next train goes at eight-thirty."

Dodge went back and bought copies of *Life*, *Judge*, and *Puck*, and frowned over the jokes; after he had read them all, he discovered that it was only quarter-past eight, and then he went out and walked up and down in front of the closed gate; he wondered if it was a card-party, and pictured them playing three at one table, or getting in some unwilling elderly member of the family who did n't know the game, to torture the other players. He could see the unhappy substitute dragged from the quiet enjoyment of an evening paper, throwing down the left bower, and then hurriedly exclaiming: "Oh, I beg your pardon, I never can remember that is a trump."

Dodge was aroused from his meditations by the sound of the last bell, which bespoke the departure of the eight-thirty train, and, dashing through the gate, he jumped aboard just as the train began to move out of the station.

He was the last guest to arrive, and as he descended to greet his hostess, he became aware of the fact that the young people were enjoying a game of blind man's buff; he also noticed that he was apparently the only man present attired in a dress suit; the perception of this fact did not tend to put him greatly at his ease, but he nevertheless endeavored to enter into the game with great enthusiasm, the result of this being his immediate capture, after which he was blindfolded and left to dash wildly about with his arms extended in the air. He fell over chairs and crickets, and struck his head against the sharp corners of bookcases and jutting cabinets laden with bric-à-brac, while the fun ran high and everybody danced about and jeered at him, and the other fellows jerked his coat tails.

By the time he had captured somebody it was announced that everybody was to adjourn to the kitchen for some magnificent fun. There were chestnuts to be roasted, apples to be pared, and endless other delightful things to be done.

In the centre of the kitchen stood a tub half-filled with water. "How jolly, we are going to bob for apples!" somebody cried out.

"Have you ever tried it, Mr. Dodge?" a sprightly young girl at his elbow asked, seeing him look curiously at the wash-tub.

He replied that he had not. "Oh, Mr. Dodge

has never bobbed for apples!" she exclamed; "we must make him begin."

"Thank you, but I think I'll let somebody else show me first," he protested, determined not to indulge, if he could possibly help it.

"Yes, Mr. Dodge had better not try it in his dress suit," put in some thoughtful member of the company; and after that, there was nothing left for him to do but to insist upon bobbing for the kind of fruit which he specially disliked, to prove that his dress suit was only an old one, which he would rather spoil than not. He was instructed that the floating apples were to be extracted from the water by the victim's teeth, and intent upon not seeming disagreeable, he ducked his head desperately into the tub and splashed and spluttered with the others. "Fortune favors the brave," and showers them with things they do not want, and this, without doubt, accounted for Dodge's well-deserved success, for he finally succeeded in extracting a much bitten apple with which he emerged dripping and wrathful, but determined not to show the white feather, even if he were asked to dance in a coal-bin.

Then followed apple act number two; this time an apple was suspended from a string, and all jumped wildly in the air after it, as if the loss of a couple of front teeth was a secondary consideration compared with the pleasure to be derived from securing a bite of that apple. Dodge and a fellow opposite him jumped for it at the same moment, and the result was a violent collision which nearly broke both their noses.

Next, some one produced a candle which was to be blown out, and the girls took turns standing upon a chair and holding it up at arms length, while the young men jumped vigorously up and down, try- ing to extinguish it with frantic puffs. Dodge, being not very tall, exerted himself manfully until he was fairly covered with candle wax, but he blew the can- dle out and nearly upset the chair, young lady and all, at the same time.

After this, they experimented with a bowl of flour and a ring, and Dodge was, of course, the unlucky one to take up the ring with his teeth from the midst of the suffocating white particles, of which he inhaled a sufficient quantity to almost choke him to death.

One of the young ladies found a dish-cloth to dust him off with, and was so kind about helping him to dispose of the superfluous flour that he was led to commit the folly of running around to the cellar door on the sly, when she started down the stairs with a looking-glass and candle.

Several of the fellows called after him that there were three steps down into the cellar, but he did not hear them, and tumbled down all three; the sudden crash frightened the young lady dreadfully, and she dropped her looking-glass and candle, and proceeded to fall down the remainder of the cellar stairs, turning her ankle, so that Dodge had the satisfaction of carrying her up the whole flight. This would have been quite romantic if he had not discovered that she was engaged to one of the other men, who had intended going around to the cellar door himself, until Dodge cut in ahead of him; moreover, she was very angry because the looking-glass was broken, and said that she should now have nothing but bad luck for seven years.

By this time, the chestnuts which had been put on the top of the stove burned up, instead of popping as they should have done, and it was discovered that nobody had thought to cut the necessary slits in them. This filled the kitchen with black smoke, which set everybody coughing, although they all declared these little mishaps were half the fun. Dodge wondered when the other half was going to begin, as he tried to remove from his knees the traces of his encounter with the cellar steps, with a sooty brush which he found hanging near the stove.

Then it was suggested that one of the most satisfactory things to do was to fill one's mouth with water and run around the house; this was a sure way of summoning one's fate in spiritual form. Dodge was so glad to fill his lungs with a little fresh air after breathing in an atmosphere of chestnuts in a state of cremation for twenty minutes, that he volunteered to make a circuit of the house among the first. He started off briskly into the wet grass, regardless of his patent leathers, and was making remarkably good time when he was suddenly stopped by an intervening clothes-line, which caught him under the chin and threw him heavily to the ground. He went quietly back to the house, thinking that if a rope around his neck was to be his fate it was not necessary to mention the lamentable fact, and he had the satisfaction of seeing the next man measure his length in the same way. Number two, however, had not the sense to keep quiet about it, but called out loudly, and applied several uncomplimentary adjectives to the clothes-line, thereby spoiling any subsequent fun in that direction.

Being all thoroughly chilled by this time, they went back and cracked nuts and pared apples, and threw the peel over their shoulders; and one girl that he had taken a special dislike to, insisted that her peel formed a perfect D, "did anybody's name that she knew begin with a D?" she inquired. Nobody could think of anybody whose name began with that letter, and Dodge tried to back quietly into the china closet, but just then somebody looked at him and giggled, and then all the others took in the situation and looked away from him, so as not to make him feel conscious, and began to talk about something else, while he blushed and tried to pretend that his interest in cracking

nuts had prevented his hearing the previous conversation.

Later they went back into the dining-room, and
had lemonade and more apples and nuts, and all said
how much nicer this simple, informal kind of thing
was, than any stereotyped supper.  Dodge was almost starved, but he contented himself with paring
another apple, and then chopping it up into small
pieces and distributing it over his plate.  The
crowning event was a Hallowe'en cake, which contained a ring, a bodkin, a piece of money, and other
appropriate tokens.

Dodge got the thimble in his slice, and nearly
swallowed it by mistake, he was so hungry; he tried
to make believe that he thought this a capital joke,
but he refrained from eating any more of the cake,
feeling sure that he had already unwittingly swallowed the button, which all were anxiously searching
for, and which nobody could seem to find.

A silvery stroke from an adjacent clock warned
him that it was time to depart, and he rose, thank-
fully, to say good-night.

" I shall always remember my first Hallowe'en
party," he protested, as he tore himself away from
the festivities, amid regrets that he must hurry off
so soon.

The silvery-toned clock turned out to be five
minutes slow, but, by running all the way to the
station, Dodge managed to swing himself on to the

platform of the rear car of the departing train, at the risk of breaking his neck. When he reached the city, he wearily entered the railroad café, and indulged in an oyster stew; it was a poor one, and the oysters therein seemed to have clung persistently to their shells, and faithfully retained fragments thereof, but Dodge meditated, philosophically, that he might as well swallow oyster shells as buttons.

As he was hurrying to recitation next morning, he met Thornton on the steps. "How was the party?" he called out; "anything like what you have in New York?"

"No, thank heaven," Dodge responded, "we may be awfully degraded there, but we have n't fallen quite so low yet."

These were the recollections that rose before the mind's eye of J. Turner Dodge, as he gazed at the withered geraniums in his window-box.

A couple of days later Manhattan dropped in to see him, remarking: "Oh, I say, when I got back to my room the other day, I found an invitation from Mrs. Horton for Hallowe'en, and I accepted, so we 'll have to have our theatre-party some other night. I knew it would n't make any difference to you, and, moreover, I thought you might be going to the party yourself."

"No, I declined on account of a previous engagement with you."

" Oh, come now, Dodge, I know better than that."

"Well, then, I have n't been educated up to Hallowe'en parties. There are some tastes that can't be acquired, you know; you must be born with them, like the love of Boston baked beans."

" Oh, you 're too New Yorky for anything; don't you know that these jolly informal things are twice as much fun?"

" Yes; but I 'm satisfied with half as much fun; you can have my other half."

" I believe you think you won't get anything to eat."

" I know better than that; they 'll have apples pared, and drawn and quartered, and suspended, and submerged, and named, and numbered, and gnawed; and chestnuts, and bodkins, and buttons, and lots of lovely things; but, in spite of all that, I prefer to be excused from parlor and kitchen gymnastics, they 're too great a strain upon my nervous system."

" All right, I 'll mention that fact to them, if they inquire about you."

" Thank you, I wish you would; and if they pin you down more particularly," Dodge concluded, " you can say to them that the truth was I 'd just got in my new football rig, and I could n't bear to spoil it."

**THE END.**

www.ingramcontent.com/pod-product-compliance
Lightning Source LLC
Chambersburg PA
CBHW030732280326
41926CB00086B/1184